MURDER BY THE BOOK

MURDER
BY THE
BOOK

THE CRIME THAT SHOCKED
DICKENS'S LONDON

Claire Harman

ALFRED A. KNOPF

New York | 2019

THIS IS A BORZOI BOOK
PUBLISHED BY ALFRED A. KNOPF

Copyright © 2018 by Claire Harman

www.aaknopf.com

Library of Congress Cataloging-in-Publication Data
Names: Harman, Claire, author.
Title: Murder by the book : the crime that shocked
Dickens's London / Claire Harman.
Description: First American edition. |
New York : Alfred A. Knopf, 2019. |
"This is a Borzoi Book." | Includes
bibliographical references and index.
Identifiers: LCCN 2018029773 (print) | LCCN 2018043723
(ebook) | ISBN 9780525520405 (ebook) |
ISBN 9780525520399 (hardcover : alk. paper)
Subjects: LCSH: Murder—England—London. | Courvoisier,
François Benjamin, —1840—Trials, litigation, etc. | Russell,
William, Lord, 1767–1840. | Ainsworth, William Harrison,
1805–1882. Jack Sheppard. | Murder in literature.
Classification: LCC HV6535.G6 (ebook) | LCC HV6535.G6
L6366 2019 (print) | DDC 364.152/3092—dc23
LC record available at https://lccn.loc.gov/2018029773

Jacket image: (book) © Alex Mit/Shutterstock
Jacket design by Janet Hansen

Manufactured in the United States of America
First American Edition

There is often in effects what was never entered into intention . . .

—*EXAMINER,* 12 JULY 1840

Contents

MURDER BY THE BOOK

Introduction

EARLY IN THE MORNING OF WEDNESDAY, 6 MAY 1840, ON an ultra-respectable Mayfair street one block to the east of Park Lane, a footman called Daniel Young answered the door to a panic-stricken young woman, Sarah Mancer, the maid of the house opposite. Fetch a surgeon, fetch a constable, she cried: her master, Lord William Russell, was lying in bed with his throat cut.

It was thought at first to be a suicide—that is what the young Queen was told at noon—but later that day, when her Secretary of State for the Colonies, Lord John Russell, arrived at Buckingham Palace, it was with the melancholy news that his uncle had in fact been murdered, his throat cut so deeply that the windpipe was sliced right through and the head almost severed. The motive appeared to be robbery, as the drawing room of Lord William's house had been turned upside down and a pile of valuables had been discovered near the front door. But the brutality of the crime was what struck the twenty-year-old monarch: "This is really too horrid!" she wrote in her diary. "It is almost an unparalleled thing for a person of Ld William's rank, to be killed like that."

Lord William's rank did indeed make him a notable corpse, however quiet and unobjectionable a live man he had been. Third and youngest son of the Marquess of Tavistock, he had passed the thirty years since the death of his wife mostly in travel and connoisseurship. He was known at the great salons of Holland House and Gore House, the Royal Academy and at the palace itself, but his status and means were nothing to those of his nephew Francis, the 7th Duke of Bedford (owner of Woburn Abbey and its priceless art collection), nor of his nephew Lord John Russell, who was one of the most influential politicians in the land. The house in Norfolk Street where Lord William lived alone was modest by Mayfair standards and he kept only three servants, a maid, a cook and a valet. Two other employees, a coachman and a groom, lived off the premises.

Who would want to butcher in his sleep this unobtrusive minor aristocrat, with his afternoons at the club and his restrained widower habits? In the newspaper articles that were about to appear, no one could find much to say about Lord William's "placid and benignant" life and "unoffending days" as a Continental traveller and absentee MP. "Aged and respected" he was called in *The Times*, like a cheese.

But as details emerged of the murder and the bungled burglary that seemed to have provoked it, fears grew that they might be symptoms of something more widespread and insidious. For, if such a person as Lord William was not safe in his bed, in the most exclusive and privileged residential enclave in the country, who could be? Such was the panic provoked by the crime, one newspaper declared, that "many families at the west-end, and more particularly aged persons living as the deceased had done in comparative retirement, entertain, perhaps for the first time, a feeling of insecurity."

These were nervous times for the ruling classes. London in 1840 was teeming with immigrants, the unemployed, and

a burgeoning working class who were more literate and organized than ever before. The winter just past had been one of
mass rallies by Chartists demanding universal suffrage that in
some places had turned into bloody riots, and Lord Brougham
had warned at the opening of Parliament in January that the
country might in fact be on the brink of revolution, so marked
was the change taking place in the disposition of the common people towards "all men in power." When over two hundred Chartist demonstrators were arrested and twenty-one
found guilty of high treason after an uprising in Newport on
4 November 1839, the ancient and barbaric punishment of
death by being hung, drawn and quartered seemed suitable
to make an example of those convicted.[*]

Was Lord William Russell's murder informed by the same
"unfortunate spirit of insubordination," as Queen Victoria
described it? Class boundaries were changing rapidly; had he
been chosen as a victim for what he represented as much as
what he owned?

The crime soon had all of London talking, from the
thieves' dens of Soho to Buckingham Palace itself, and for
the first time, perhaps, politicians weren't the only people
being blamed for undermining the status quo and stirring up
a volatile underclass. As the investigation into Lord William
Russell's death proceeded, several of the leading writers of
the day were alarmed to find themselves suddenly under fire
for having contributed to what *The Monthly Review* charac-
terized as a "general want of settledness" by writing fictions
that glamorized vice and made heroes of criminals. Given the
chance to mould the taste of a mass audience, many of them

---

[*] The sentences were commuted to transportation for life, a sign of leni-
ency that also seems to have been a sign of nervousness.

were now accused of pandering to the lowest, with books full of violent excitements and vulgarity that could all too easily lead susceptible readers astray.

One bestselling book in particular did more than any other to inflame this panic about "low" culture, but to see how closely it was linked to the gory events in Norfolk Street, we need to return to the evening of Lord William's murder and follow his movements in his last hours of life.

A Last Walk

AT SIX O'CLOCK ON THE EVENING OF 5 MAY 1840, A SPARE old gentleman of medium height and distinguished but unshowy appearance could have been seen walking a large white dog along Norfolk Street in Mayfair, just a few yards away from Hyde Park's north-east corner. He didn't go far, nor proceed very fast: Lord William Russell was asthmatic and suffered from a hernia that made walking difficult. He was heading towards a house just off Grosvenor Square, to combine a message for an upholsterer, Mr. Barry, with his routine airing before dinner.

He was not in the best of moods, having had to reprimand his valet an hour earlier for forgetting to send the carriage to the club. What use was keeping a carriage if you had to come home in a hackney cab? The whole business of maintaining an address in London was bothersome, much more trouble than the old life of moving from place to place on the Continent, living for long periods in the houses of friends or relations, or staying in hotels. But his travelling days were over. "I feel too old," he had told his nephew three years earlier, "and have at last made up—to set down quietly in London like an old Hack—turned out to grass for life."

The place where he had settled, a terraced townhouse at

14 Norfolk Street,[*] was a far cry from Woburn Abbey, the
family home of the Russells, where Lord William had been
brought up and where, until his death in 1839, his elder
brother, John, had kept one of the most splendid private resi-
dences in the country, after the Queen's. John's son Francis
had now succeeded to the dukedom and the grand estate, and
positions in the family had shifted once more, pushing Lord
William a little further from the centre of power and money.
Grandson of one duke, brother to the next two, and uncle to
the latest, Lord William was doomed to be a satellite male in
a family well provided with heirs, and as such of small fortune and no importance. Even his name seemed to belong to
him a little less as the years went by, and he was now referred
to as "*old* Lord William" to distinguish him from his nephew,
a well-known diplomat.

There had been advantages, of course, to existing on the
perimeters of a great and powerful clan: as long as he didn't
develop outrageous habits and run up disproportionate debts,
Lord William had always been protected by family cash and
welcomed at the ducal home. Family patronage assured him
the seat in Parliament that he held for four elections from the
age of twenty-two, but it was just as well that his charming
bride, Charlotte Villiers (eldest daughter of the Earl of Jersey), had had a fortune of her own. They married in the year
of the French Revolution, 1789, and lived abroad for much
of the time, in Italy, Germany and Switzerland. Lady Charlotte bore him seven children, four boys and three girls, and

---

[*] Norfolk Street was renamed Dunraven Street in 1939 and has been
extensively redeveloped in the years since Lord William lived there. The
old No. 14 no longer exists, but was situated on the east side of the street,
between Green Street and North Row.

her death in 1808, aged thirty-seven, stunned him. In the long decades since, Lord William always kept a miniature portrait of her, painted on ivory, in his dressing case, and until a few weeks previously had carried on his person at all times a gold locket containing a strand of his dead wife's hair. The loss of this locket on a recent visit to Richmond had upset the old man greatly. It had been his most treasured possession.

In the thirty years since Lady Charlotte's death, his habits had become increasingly solitary; he travelled a lot, studied artworks and advised his brother on which sculptures and paintings to buy for the seemingly endless halls of Woburn. His fine family might have been a comfort to him, but three of his four sons died young: the second eldest, Captain George Russell RN, died of fever in the West Indies in 1825; the eldest, Francis, a promising soldier, became addicted to gambling, ending "an inglorious life," as the 6th Duke lamented, among racecourse ruffians in 1832; and John, the third son, a commander in the navy, died on active service three years later. Of his three daughters, one had died in infancy and his eldest child, Gertrude, lived abroad under the shadow of chronic illness ("a little deranged," the Prime Minister, Lord Melbourne, thought). Thus of Lord William's seven offspring only two remained close by: his younger daughter Eliza, who had been brought up at Woburn by her uncle and aunt and had married her cousin; and his only remaining son, Mr. William Russell, Attorney General of the Duchy of Lancaster (known as "Counsellor William" in the family).

Lord William's eccentricities and absent-mindedness were often remarked on, and as he made his way towards Grosvenor Square on his evening walk, he was very likely talking to himself, or the dog. One of the servants had called him a "rum old chap" recently, and it was true: when he lived abroad and heard that the younger Russells were likely to visit, he typically went somewhere else, happy to be rattling round Europe alone in his post-chaise, which "I have for very many years found a very pleasant home and I am thankful for it as it has furnished me opportunity for reflection and Philosophy." He was most at home these days at his clubs, Brooks's on St. James's Street and the Travellers on Pall Mall, and seldom entertained in Norfolk Street. His servants must have got used to it being a quiet and predictable place, with Lord William alone in the study among his prints and paintings, the clock ticking and the fire waxing and waning. It was all too quiet for the cook, Mary Hannell, who had recently given notice, desiring a change. She was going to forget how to do her job, she said, if she stayed any longer with his Lordship.

Why Lord William had spent so many of his seventy-two years abroad is not entirely clear. The Continent was the usual refuge for those who had fallen on hard times, or were evading their creditors; it was also a place where one could sit out a scandal. Any of those reasons could have held true for Lord William in a period of his life which he looked back on as "abundantly full of vexation." Florence, Rome, Bologna, Leghorn, Geneva, Paris: we see him flitting through other people's letters and journals in the 1820s and 1830s, staying in hotels, or—more frequently—at someone else's house, Lady Hardy's or the Abercorns', the Payne-Galways' or the Fitzclarences', or being gathered into the Earl and Countess of Blessington's circle when that notorious "circus" arrived in Genoa. It comes as a surprise to find that this eccentric solitary took part enthusiastically in masquerade balls and made an impressive Sir Peter Teazle (the plum part) in an amateur production of *School for Scandal* put on at Lord Burghersh's in the summer of 1823, in which Lady Hardy played Mrs.

Candour. "I have heard that he acted very well and that you *looked* very well," Byron teased her.

Lady Hardy, the wife of Nelson's right-hand man at Trafalgar, was one of Lord William's more observant friends, noting his old-fashioned gallantry towards her and Lady Westmorland and his habit of buttonholing people at parties. She thought him "as odd and absent as ever" in 1825, and on an excursion to Chamonix he amused and slightly disconcerted the ladies present by "jumping and hopping about like the boys who were with us . . . He took off his Coat and capered about in his waistcoat holding his staff to jump over the *crévasses*." Lady Hardy didn't consider Lord William the remarrying type, and noticed more than he might have wished. When he was visiting her in Lausanne in September 1822, he had developed the peculiar habit of putting his watch in his mouth as he paced up and down the room. One morning he announced that he had lost this watch and suspected his manservant of having stolen it, which Lady Hardy tried to persuade him was unlikely (the servant being a highly respectable one). "You swallowed it in one of your absent fits," she said as a joke, at which Lord William stopped and said, "Do you really think so? *It is possible*." "Most certainly it was not," Lady Hardy wrote tartly in her diary, "as it had a Gold chain and Seal attached to it which never could have got down his throat even if his huge watch had." She made some discreet enquiries via the servants as to where Lord William might have mislaid his watch, and discovered that he had recently "taken several warm baths at a questionable establishment in the Cité of Lausanne, where it was not advisable for Ladies to go." This was undoubtedly where he and the timepiece had parted company, she concluded.

Were such "questionable establishments" Lord William's

frequent haunts? In his diary of 1829, his nephew William
(who was fond of him) lamented Uncle Bill's "strange mode
of life, neither respectable nor useful," and to Lady Holland
described him as "an unhappy wandering spirit" who "wan-
ders about from tavern to tavern without knowing why or
wherefore." There seems something unacknowledged here,
either a temperamental quirk or a vice.

Lord William's private life necessarily remains private,
but one possible cause of the "vexation" which propelled him
and his wife abroad in 1807 might perhaps be detected in a
piece of gossip passed on to the teenage Queen Victoria in the
first year of her reign by her confidant and mentor, Lord Melbourne. The late Lady William Russell, Melbourne told Victoria, "had a great connection and friendship with the Duke of
Argyll." "She was sister to the Duchess of Argyll," the Queen
recorded in her diary, "but Lord M. said he didn't marry the
latter till Lady William died." This is tantamount to saying
that Lady William and the Duke had been lovers, though the
situation may have been even more complicated than that,
since Argyll's wife after 1810, Lady William's sister Caroline,
had to divorce her husband, William Paget, in order to marry
him, so the Duke may have been involved with both married Villiers sisters simultaneously. It would partly account
for what Elizabeth Wynne wrote in her diary in 1807, in a
very rare glimpse of the married life of Lord William and
Lady Charlotte, when she related how she had spent a pleasant evening at "Lady William Russell's," with the Duke of
Argyll and "a Mrs. Page" (presumably Mrs. Paget) the only
other guests. Lord William was present too, "of course," Mrs.
Wynne noted, but added this significant phrase, "*quoiqu'il me
parait un zero dans sa maison*": in other words, it appeared

to her that Lord William counted for nothing in his own household—a cuckold, in spirit if not in fact. But the question remains, was he deliberately turning a blind eye to his wife's "great connection and friendship" with Argyll, or was he the kind of cuckold who hadn't even noticed anything going on?

On his walk to Grosvenor Square, Lord William turned from Green Street into Park Street, avoiding the unpaved mews and "rows" connecting the residential blocks where all the routine maintenance of Mayfair life went on and where, cheek-by-jowl with the gentry, you could find plumbers, plasterers, coal dealers, carpenters, wheelwrights and vets. Along North Row, adjacent to Norfolk Street, the nature of the trades seemed to change gradually west to east, from the City of Norwich public house at the corner, past a shoemaker, a grocer's shop and two livery stables (one, Shenton's, where Lord William kept his carriage, and where the dog went to sleep at night), past a tailor and hairdresser to some less genteel businesses at the eastern end of the lane: a beer shop, a corn dealer, a bottle shop and a rag man.

Walking along Park Street took him past the house of his friend Lady Julia Lockwood, Lady Abercorn's sister and a close associate of Lady Hardy. She had recently helped Lord William out of a domestic difficulty when his trusted valet, an Englishman called James Ellis, gave notice to go and work for the Earl of Mansfield. Lord William complained about this to Lady Julia, and she told him that a former footman of hers, a young Swiss, was on the lookout for a new position. Lord William wrote to the boy's employer, John Minet Fector (MP for Maidstone), and the deal was soon done. Lord

William saved some money by getting a junior servant on a probationary salary, and the footman got a promotion, a significant raise and a move to central London.

There seems to have been something of a vogue for Swiss servants at the time: difficult employment conditions in their homeland in the years following the disbanding of the national army were perhaps encouraging Swiss workers to migrate, and English middle- and upper-class households at this date were insatiably hungry for domestic staff. In Lord William's circle, the Swiss were liked for being cheap, clean and reliable. Sir Robert Adair had a Swiss servant, as did Lady Hardy, and Lady Julia had two, Henri Pethoud and his wife Jeanne, who had both known Mr. Fector's boy since his arrival in England four years earlier, and were friends with his uncle (both were called Courvoisier), now butler to Sir George Beaumont.

The hiring and keeping of servants was a constant topic of concern among the circles in which Lord William lived and moved. Turnover rates were high, disasters frequent and employers got used to being constantly on the lookout for good recommendations from friends. When Lord William was about to go travelling in 1831, he enquired of his nephew William about a "stupid old Swiss" called Girardet whom they'd had in service the year before, and subsequently took him on. It worked out fairly well while the two were on the road (Girardet proved a very comforting nurse during a chest infection), but in England Lord William found him "absolutely useless—of more plague than profit." He wished he had kept the "intelligent and honest" German he'd had the year before, though *his* culpable shortcoming had been a rough and unfeeling manner. Lord William, it seems, was quite hard to please on this score.

The new boy, François Courvoisier, who was coming from a large and lavish establishment near Dover, may not have understood how much was included in the job of "manservant" in a small household such as Lord William's, with responsibility for maintaining his master's wardrobe, brushing clothes and hats, helping him shave, dress and undress, attending to his hair, polishing boots and shoes and keeping all his accessories clean and ready to wear. The valet at Norfolk Street also had the duties of a butler and was expected to serve his master meals and keep the silver polished. In addition, as the only male domestic, he would inevitably be called on to do small handyman tasks all the time and the heavy lifting of coals and water. A valet also needed to have excellent powers of understanding and discretion, and the Swiss boy was neither very well educated nor a very sophisticated speaker of English. A decade later, in her bestselling book on household management, Isabella Beeton identified the pitfalls when trying to get such services on the cheap, saying that while valets were given the responsibility of being "the confidants and agents of their [masters'] most unguarded moments, of their most secret habits," the servants themselves were rarely equal to the task, "being subject to erring judgement, aggravated by an imperfect education."

But these considerations were overlooked when Lord William acquired his new valet on 1 April. What a pity that the boy was too stupid to remember all his messages, necessitating this extra call to the upholsterer. He crossed Grosvenor Square to its south-east corner and rang the bell at 1 Charles Street, where he asked Mr. Barry to wait on him at home as soon as possible. Then Lord William turned round and set off immediately back to Norfolk Street. The dog must have been disappointed.

It was a pleasant late spring evening when they got home, with the sun lighting the window boxes on the first floor, which were full of geraniums and fragrant mignonette. Fourteen Norfolk Street was a typical early nineteenth-century London townhouse, with three main storeys and a narrow frontage of about fifteen feet. The front door led into a passage off which was a dining room (at the front) and a cloakroom beyond it, with a water closet beyond that; through a half-glazed back door a flight of external steps took you down into the yard. On the first floor there was a drawing room at the front, overlooking the street, and behind that a small sitting room or study. Lord William's bedroom was at the front on the next floor up, with an unused spare room connected to it, and up the attic stairs (sealed off with a door) were the servants' bedrooms, the maid and cook sharing the room at the front, with a lumber room connected to it, and the valet on his own in a small and rather cramped chamber at the back. Outside at the front of the house, a gated railing and steps led down to the "area," where you entered the kitchen, scullery and butler's pantry. There was a back door from the pantry into the yard, which had high walls on each side and abutted other properties in each direction.

It was a house full of pictures and small antiquities. Lord William's latest acquisition had been a print titled "The Vision of Ezekiel" that he had bought from Moltino's in Pall Mall just the previous week. Ellis, his former valet (who could be trusted with such a task), had come by specially to hang it the previous day, and the small stepladder he had used was still in the yard, waiting to be put away.

Lord William went upstairs to change for dinner, and when Mr. Barry arrived a few minutes later he was asked to wait in the dining room. Presently, Barry heard the big dog's footsteps preceding his master down the stairs. "I left him in good health and spirits with the dog," the tradesman said later, believing he was probably the last person, apart from the servants of the house, to see Lord William alive.

Lord William dined alone as usual at seven and spent the evening in his study on the first floor, reading the newly published memoirs of Sir Samuel Romilly, the Whig legal reformer, whom he had known. William York, the coachman, came to the house a little before nine to fetch the dog back to the livery stables on North Row, and the valet and maid supped together in the kitchen just after that. The cook, Mary Hannell, had gone out for the evening to see a friend, but on her return she came to the front door, not the servants' entrance, and the valet, who let her in, confirmed that he had locked, chained and bolted that door as usual afterwards.

The first of the servants to go up to bed was Sarah Mancer, the maid, who saw the light on under the door of the room where his Lordship was reading. Her last job of the day was to light a fire in his bedroom, as he always had one (and a warming pan, which it was the valet's duty to provide), even in summer. All those years in southern Europe must have made Lord William particularly sensitive to the cold and damp of London. She placed a thin rushlight ready by his bed and went on up to the room in the attic that she shared with the cook. Lord William's door was baize-covered and had a spring on it which made it "close of itself," without a noise. The bell-hanger's man had just mended the door handle, and earlier in the day the bell-pull over the bed had also been fixed.

The cook had her supper of cold meat and beer and went up to bed about half an hour later, possibly a little the worse for drink, as she slept extremely heavily that night. She had left the fire burning in the kitchen, and some extra coals, alongside the warming pan.

At about 11:50 p.m., the bell rang from the study: Lord William was going up to bed, late as ever. The valet filled the warming pan with hot coals from the pantry fire and took it up to the bedroom. He helped his master to bed, lit the rush-light and also, at his Lordship's request, a candle so that he could carry on reading. Though there was a key on the inside of the door, his Lordship never locked it. Everything in the chamber was as it should be; the valet went to bed.

The street was quiet. Two Metropolitan Police constables, Alfred Slade and George Glew, passed along it several times during the night, one on each side, and reported nothing unusual. The smart new Peelers had taken over some of the duties of the old "street-keepers" and so, as he passed 14 Norfolk Street, Glew tested the front door, and was later able to confirm it had been locked.

But in the middle of the night, two of the neighbours were alerted to something unusual going on. At around 2 a.m., Louisa Anstruther, the married daughter of Lord William's immediate neighbour, Sir Howard Elphinstone, heard something through the bedroom wall that adjoined her own room, a groan or cry. She thought no more about it at the time and went back to sleep.

And across the road, a gentleman visitor at number 23 saw an extraordinary thing through one of the windows opposite, flitting across his line of vision, something that looked like the figure of a naked man. Perhaps this struck him as amusing at the time—someone else engaged in clandestine nocturnal activities, like himself. Though, of course, he wasn't meant to have seen anything, wasn't meant to be in Norfolk Street at all, visiting his married mistress in the middle of the night. He, too, put the incident out of his mind.

But at seven in the morning, Henry Lakes, the footman at number 22, was cleaning shoes below stairs when the bell rang furiously. By the time he got up the area steps, the caller had run on to the house next door. It was the housemaid from number 14, screaming at Mr. Latham's man, Daniel Young, about the house being robbed and her master dead. Somehow that night, mayhem and murder had come to their street.

2

The Crime

THAT FIRST HALF HOUR AFTER THE DISCOVERY OF LORD William's body was one of utter confusion. No one knew whom to send for, or in what order to do things. The commotion had brought several other servants out from the neighbouring houses, but there wasn't a policeman in sight, so the two footmen Lakes and Young set off in different directions to find a constable, then hurried back to Norfolk Street, where York, Lord William's coachman, had been fetched from the mews. The other servants were all clustered downstairs in number 14, the valet sitting with his head in his hands and seemingly in shock, and when Young said should they go and see how his Lordship was, all he did was moan, "Oh no, I cannot; no, I cannot; oh my poor Lord; he's murdered, he's murdered!" So Young and York went upstairs without him and in the front bedroom found Lord William's body lying in the bed with the covers drawn up and a small towel covering its face. The left hand, which was gripping the sheet, was quite cold, and there was blood on the pillow, blood all through the bed and pooled on the floor beneath it.

When Police Constables John Baldwin and William Rose got to the house, they found the female servants in hysterics but the valet sitting on a chair in the dining room, seemingly overcome by inertia. He had begun writing a note to his master's son in Cheshunt Place, infuriating the maid, who had told him they should be sending a messenger on a horse as fast as possible; she had been so frustrated at his lack of initiative that she had shouted at the valet, and pushed him. Baldwin also couldn't get any sense out of the young man: he asked him twice why he was sitting doing nothing, but didn't get an answer.

Inspector John Tedman of C Division (covering Mayfair and Soho) was the first officer on the scene and spoke to the servants briefly downstairs before going to look at the corpse. He removed the towel that had been so strangely placed over the face, turned back the bedclothes and saw "a great quantity of blood in the bed, from his lordship's head down to the middle." The nearest doctor, a Mr. Henry Elsgood of Park Street, had been called in and gave the opinion that Lord William had been dead for three to four hours. The wound to the neck was brutal, a huge gash five inches deep and seven inches long, extending from the cervical vertebrae to the shoulder, inflicted very cleanly and with considerable force by "some sharp instrument" (not found) and made from the left while the body was lying to the right. It had divided the trachea and would have caused instant death, Elsgood reported. Half an hour later, at about eight o'clock, Lord William's regular doctor, John Nussey of Cleveland Row, arrived and gave a rather different view of the time of death: he said it had occurred six to seven hours previously. He also noticed that the ball of the right thumb was cut off, which he took as a sign that Lord William had tried to defend himself. He was categorical about ruling out any possibility of suicide, given the depth and nature of the wound and the fact that the victim's face had been covered, not to mention the lack of any obvious motive on Lord William's part.

Nussey was able to confirm that the victim had been a physically frail man and "very deaf," also that he suffered from a hernia and habitually wore a truss, and that "from the position the truss was found in, in my opinion he had had some slight struggle." The blood-soaked truss was presumably what Daniel Young described later as a "dark handkerchief" lying underneath Lord William's body when he was asked to help search the bed. Tedman and his colleague Inspector Henry Beresford had meanwhile been examining the room in which the corpse lay. The two razors used for the daily shave were still in their box, without the slightest mark on either, and no other weapon could be found; all the household's carving knives were clean and in their proper places downstairs. An empty dressing case was open on the bed and a Russian leather coin box was next to it, opened and emptied. There was a book and a pair of spectacles on the floor, a burnt-out candle on the bookcase between the windows and a partially burned rushlight on the nightstand. Tedman asked the valet, was anything missing? Yes, the gold watch from Lord William's watchstand, at least five of his Lordship's rings, at least £15 from the note case and some gold coins. He wasn't sure what else. Quite a lot of valuables remained in the room: silver dressing articles; a gold-handled cane; a gold pin; and a miniature portrait of a lady, painted on ivory, that lay next to the dressing case on the bed, inanimate witness to the bloody crime.

Being in the room with the corpse was distressing, and the valet kept sitting down and moaning, or running off to get drinks of water. Daniel Young had felt similarly traumatized

by the gruesome spectacle in the four-poster: "It was very horrifying, so much as to affect the nerves of the stoutest, stron-
gest man—it certainly affected me." The maid had been quite
overcome after discovering the body, and the cook said she
had not been able to look properly, but just got as far as the
bottom of the bed, and then had to run away to the kitchen.

It was presumed that the assailant, or gang of assailants,
had got into the house through the rear yard, for there were
bruises on the back door, and one of the bolts had fallen off.
The bureau in the drawing room and the sideboard in the
dining room had their drawers turned out, and the press in
the pantry (where the silver plate and cutlery were usually
kept) had been wrenched open with a tool. Several small gold
and silver items had been abandoned by the thieves, wrapped
in one of Lord William's cloaks and left in a bundle by the
front door (including a silver thimble, which turned out to
belong to the cook and which she said she had put away in
her workbox the evening before). Other valuable silverware
seemed to be missing, although without checking the inventory it was impossible to say how much.

The pantry window, which the valet had secured the previous night, was found to be unfastened and, as he pointed
out, there was a ladder in the yard, used by James Ellis two
days before to hang Lord William's new picture. The butler
from number 15, Thomas Selway, obligingly inspected the
top of the adjoining wall from the other side to see if there
were any signs of escape there, but the dust wasn't at all disturbed (and was so thick "even a cat's foot would have left
a mark"); Constables Baldwin and Rose now tried climbing
on to the slates at the back of number 14, finding nothing,
while making plenty of new marks of their own. But Tedman was already wondering what sort of professional thief

would bother forcing the stout back door when there was a thin half-glazed one a short flight of steps above it, and who would throw a lot of things around a study but fail to remove so many valuable and highly portable small *objets d'art* from Lord William's collections. "No thief would ever leave this property behind," he remarked, fingering the silver dish, silver sugar dredger and gold pencil case that had been found by the door, and the valet agreed it was strange.

Before long, there were constables all over the house, horrified neighbours in the street and shocked members of Lord William's family arriving from all parts. The victim's son, Mr. William Russell, drove up first, deeply distressed; Lord William's nephew Lord John Russell followed, accompanied by Mr. Wing, the family solicitor. The celebrated artist Edwin Landseer arrived soon after. He was a great friend of William Russell and had known Lord William well for many years; he was also the long-term lover of Lord William's sister-in-law, the recently widowed Duchess of Bedford, who arrived with him; both were distraught.* Some idea of how seriously the crime was being taken was given by the prompt appearance in Norfolk Street of the two men at the very top of the Metropolitan Police hierarchy, the joint commissioners, Lieutenant Colonel Charles Rowan and Mr. Richard Mayne, and then the Home Secretary himself, the Marquess of Normanby. The house may have begun to seem rather full at this point. Later in the day Fox Maule, the Under-Secretary of State, was sent to assess the situation for the Prime Minister, Lord Melbourne, so that he could keep the Queen apprised of events.

---

* Landseer's affair with Georgiana, Duchess of Bedford, a woman twenty-one years his senior, started when he was still a teenager; he is thought to have been the father of her last two children.

Melbourne reported back to the Queen at the end of the day that the back door had been broken open, "but there were no traces of persons having approached the door from without." "It is a most mysterious affair. The bed was of course deluged with blood, but there were no marks of blood in any other part of the room." This absence of any bloodstains, apart from in the bed, was puzzling the police considerably. They had inspected all the grates in the house for signs of things having been burned—clothes or rags—and the sinks and basins for evidence of anything being washed, all to no avail. "I did not see the slightest marks of blood about any of these people, or in any part of the house," Tedman reported. "I examined all the places that I possibly could, and there was not the slightest tinge about them, on the linen, bed curtains, or any where else in any part of the house. I searched very carefully to see if there was any cutting instrument any where with which the wound might have been given, and searched every room of the house." How could Lord William's carotid artery have been hacked right through without vast amounts of blood spurting up on to the bed hangings, the bedspread, the curtains—and the murderers? And how could anyone have got away from the scene without leaving a spot or smudge behind on any surface, even on things like the emptied dressing case and coin box, which had obviously been handled after the killing?

While the family and Mr. Mayne conferred in the drawing room, Beresford took statements from the servants and searched their boxes (the only real piece of private property a servant had), but found nothing suspicious except a chisel in the valet's room, which, when he compared it with the prise-marks on the press in the pantry, fitted well. Courvoisier said it was indeed his chisel, and that he had acquired it when he

lived in Dover, for his woodworking hobby, fashioning trin-
kets out of wood and bone. He also had a purse containing a
£5 note and six sovereigns, all of which he said were his own,
the note being one his Lordship had wanted changed just a
few days previously.

Tedman inspected the lower back door, and was increasingly convinced that the marks on it had been made from
the inside, and that the burglary had been staged. "Some of you
in the house have done this deed," he said to the servants omi-
nously, to which the valet replied, "If they have I hope they will
be found out." "There is not much fear but what they will,"
Tedman countered, though privately he was feeling rather
doubtful. "I examined everything as I went along," he admitted later, "but saw nothing to tend to explain this case at all."

The inquest into Lord William's death was held promptly on
the evening of the same day at the City of Norwich public
house at the north-east corner of the street, with an interval
during which the coroner took the jurors round every part of
the house, including the bedchamber, where the victim's pal-
lid body lay (almost) undisturbed.

In her testimony to the coroner, Sarah Mancer told how
she had got up that morning at 6:30, a little earlier than usual,
but on going downstairs began to notice many things in disarray, the dining room and drawing room strewn with papers,
Lord William's davenport desk turned around and the bundle near the front door, which was unbolted and unchained.
Running up to alert Mary Hannell and Courvoisier, she
found Mary asleep, but the valet already dressed; the two of
them then went down to the basement together and found

the press forced open and the back door broken. "My God, someone has been robbing us!" Courvoisier cried. Going to tell his Lordship the alarming news, Courvoisier preceded her into the bedroom and moved immediately to the windows to open the shutters. It was left to Sarah to call out to her master around the half-closed bed curtains, but then she saw blood on the pillow—she wasn't sure what else. At that point she panicked, started screaming and ran out of the room.

The servants' statements to the coroner and the police gave a close account of what had happened the previous day. Lord William had risen at 9 a.m. as usual, breakfasted and read in his study, then went out to his club after lunch, giving instructions to the valet to send the carriage at 5 p.m. to Brooks's (a name Courvoisier hadn't recognized, but he had been in service only five weeks, two of which had been spent out of town). It was sunny, and Lord William left the house on foot, walking with a stick. Two of Mr. Barry's workmen had visited 14 Norfolk Street during the day, the first to replace the bell-pull above Lord William's bed, the second to fix its wire and the handle of his baize-lined bedroom door. The valet oversaw the first job, which took about fifteen minutes, and the maid the second, which took ten.

While the second workman was about his business, a friend of Courvoisier called Henry Carr, who had been in service with him in Dover but was currently unemployed, dropped in to see the valet and was invited to stay for tea in the kitchen. Sarah Mancer had seen Carr at least twice before, and two other men from Mr. Fector's, James Leech and William Jones, but didn't know much about any of them, Courvoisier being such a recent addition to the household. While Carr was there, the coachman, William York, came in to ask if the carriage was needed, at which point the valet realized he had forgotten Lord William's request. It was already well after five, so York went off to fetch his master. Courvoisier was in the pantry with Henry Carr when Lord William arrived home in the hackney cab, irritated at the neglect of his instructions, but keen to go for his customary pre-dinner walk, for which purpose Courvoisier was sent round to the stables in North Row to fetch the dog.

Mary Hannell confirmed that she had brought in some meat for her own supper from one of the outbuildings in the backyard later and bolted the top of the back-area door when she came in, but wasn't able to lock the bottom as the bolt had been broken for some time. Courvoisier went out once more after that (by the front-area door) to fetch her some beer from the nearby pub. This was something he'd never done before, but as the cook was about to leave the household after a stay of three years, he said he thought he'd give her a treat. On his return, he locked the front-area door, but wasn't sure about the gate at the top of the steps. He put the key back on the hook in the kitchen where it lived.

Suspicion of the valet ("the *foreigner*") had been growing during the day, but his behaviour at the inquest did much to improve his standing, and Lord John Russell reported afterwards that "the impression had been that the servant [Courvoisier] was not guilty." Now that the first shock was wearing off, he seemed appropriately sorrowful and sombre, and though the coroner reminded him that he was not obliged to say anything prejudicial to himself, Courvoisier took the oath voluntarily and was the soul of quiet obligingness, giving a sample of his handwriting without demur (to compare with some words written on the banknote in his possession) and calmly relating his last dealings with his master on Tuesday evening, how he had left him safe and well in bed and heard nothing more until the housemaid knocked at his bedroom door next morning to wake him up.

Yes, Henry Carr had called at 14 Norfolk Street on Tuesday afternoon, with a shotgun he had won in a lottery and was going to raffle later the same day, and Carr had accompanied Courvoisier part-way to the stables when he went to fetch the dog for Lord William's walk. Both men had been in the service of Mr. Fector a couple of years back, though Carr had subsequently worked for a Mrs. Green and had been unemployed for about three months. "[He] is not in reduced circumstances, to my knowledge," Courvoisier added, and "is now, I believe, to be found at the Royal Exchange public-house, Adam's-mews."

The foreman of the jury stood up at the end of the questioning to let the witness know that he had managed to speak to Mr. Fector that very day and had obtained an unimpeachable report of Courvoisier's character during the two and a half years he was in service in Dover, a testimony that seemed to impress the jury and give satisfaction to the witness, too. At the end of this long and gruelling day, the valet was taken back to 14 Norfolk Street under a police escort to join Sarah Mancer and Mary Hannell, all three of the traumatized servants kept in separate rooms in "a state of vigilance which was called by the French term *surveillance*," as one of the lawyers described it. There might well have been some sort of conspiracy between them, it was thought, or with some outside parties, and until any arrests were made Inspector Tedman, a sergeant called Pullen and a constable from C Division would sleep at the house to monitor them.

It was dark by the time the inquest concluded, with a verdict of "wilful murder against some person or persons

unknown." The street outside the City of Norwich was completely blocked with people waiting to hear the outcome,
many remaining in the area "the greater part of the night"—
no doubt to the increasing discomfort of the late Lord's neighbours: Louisa Anstruther at number 13; Mr. Cutler at number
15; and the grander houses on the west side of the street, with
a full view of all the distressing comings and goings—Mr.
Latham at number 23, the rich banker Mr. Loyd at number
22 and Sir Felix Agar at number 21. The constable on duty
outside number 14 was plagued with enquiries all night, but
maintained a rigid silence.

The murder quickly became the first topic of speculation
across the city, from the bars and dives of Soho to Mayfair's
clubs and salons, where so many people had known the victim
personally. "For a considerable number of years no event has
occurred in the metropolis that has created a greater degree of
excitement and consternation," *The Times* declared, "than the
tragical event which it now becomes our most painful duty
to record." Hundreds of people had gravitated towards Norfolk Street, including several carriage-loads of ladies, waiting
in the rain to catch whatever news emerged from the house.
Lords Cowley and Ashburnham and the Marquess of Salis-
bury had been spotted in the crowd, and several members
of the nobility had called in at the house, "for the purpose
of making enquiries as to the truth of the rumours current,
concerning the murder." One of the rumours was that "vast
property" had been stolen, for there had to be some adequate
motive.

In his dressing room at the Haymarket theatre, the great
actor William Macready was annoyed to have his prepara-

tions for a performance of *Hamlet* interrupted by "the *bruit* which is made about this poor old man's death." His *Hamlet* was just about the only serious play on in the city at the time, nine other theatres being occupied in competing stage versions of *Jack Sheppard*, a tawdry tale of thieves and cutthroats. At the other side of town, the painter Benjamin Robert Haydon had been having an excellent day in the studio (for once) when he heard the news. He had been working on a painting called *Highland Lovers:* "Never glazed better or more effectively!" he wrote in his diary, then "Poor Lord William Russell has been murdered! A strange entry in one day."

Charles Dickens, who was living nearby in Devonshire Terrace, must have followed the unfolding news with more than usual interest. He was writing a story—*Barnaby Rudge*—that begins with the brutal stabbing in his bed of the elderly Reuben Haredale, by an undiscovered intruder. Life, it seemed, was imitating art. And at his desk in Great Coram Street in Bloomsbury, the young illustrator and journalist William Makepeace Thackeray was bothered by the noise of the news-seller's cries outside: "Here is a man shouting out We shall have this Lord William Russell murder," he wrote to his mother; "a nuisance and so it is the stupid town talks about nothing else." Little did he realize how much more talk there would be in the coming months, nor how closely this crime touched his own concerns.

On the morning after the inquest, Police Commissioner Richard Mayne was back at Norfolk Street instigating a thorough search of the house, particularly the servants' rooms, while "scientific persons" were called in to inspect the door frames with magnifying glasses. The knives used in the household all seemed intact and unstained (except one carving knife, which had a possible mark on it), but in order to ascertain whether or not a weapon had been disposed of, the two water closets were to be dismantled and the drains inspected; even the cesspool would be sieved, and the roof and guttering were also to be searched. It was just possible that the murderer could have broken in during the day on Tuesday and hidden in the house, waiting for everyone to go to bed. A nimble person might have done so while the valet was out fetching the beer: "even that short interval would have been quite sufficient for a man on the watch to go down the area-steps, and conceal himself on the premises until the hour arrived for putting into execution his dreadful design," *The Times* surmised. And it couldn't be entirely ruled out that the intruder or intruders were still hiding somewhere—up the chimneys, perhaps, or in the coal hole. Sweeps were called in to flush out all the house's darkest crannies.

All this time, Lord William's body remained upstairs. The blood-soaked mattresses had been removed and destroyed as soon as the inquest jury had viewed the room on the evening of the 6th, when the corpse had also been cleaned up and laid out. It was quite usual at that date for a corpse to be kept at home between death and funeral, laid out in an open coffin (weather permitting) for a week, during which time people could come and pay their respects. An enterprising *Times* journalist who had gained access to Lord William's house on Thursday 7 May was pleased to report that the chin had been tied up, and a white cloth placed around the throat, "by which means the fatal wound is now hidden from view." "Yesterday the features of his Lordship presented no traces of his violent death, but the calmness and placidity of sleep."

The journalist had already heard rumours that the servants across the road were privy to some delicate information which might have a bearing on the case, "some circumstance on the evening preceding the murder which has since struck them as bearing a suspicious appearance; but we understand that at present they decline stating what it was that attracted their attention." The reason given was "a fear that they might implicate some party against whom no previous suspicion attached," but the paper hoped the police wouldn't allow false delicacy to stand in the way of justice and that whatever had been noticed would soon be made public. This seems to be the first hint of the "naked man" story which keeps cropping up, in increasingly bizarre forms, at the edges of accounts of the murder. Some of Mr. Latham's servants—or perhaps *Mrs.* Latham's servants—must have been fully aware of their mistress's adulterous affair and seem to have been advised not to set off a different sort of investigation altogether, unless it became absolutely necessary.

Fourteen Norfolk Street was a very full building that morning: the female servants were being kept in the attic; the valet was being held in the dining room, while one floor above him members of the Russell family, including the Duke of Bedford and Lord John, were holding another meeting with Mayne and the Marquess of Normanby to set up a private enquiry into the murder alongside the official one, helped by a lawyer known to them, Francis Hobler, who had offered his services gratis. With so little forthcoming about who might be responsible for the crime, they had decided to offer a reward for information, the considerable sum of £400,[*] half of which

---

[*] The sum of £400 was what the Governor of the Bank of England earned annually at the time, and about ten times the average manservant's income.

would be put up by the family and half by the government (this was at the Queen's request). Posters were ordered immediately, to be placed all over the city.

The inventory showed that besides some of the small valuables from the bedroom, there were at least fourteen pieces of silver cutlery and some larger silverware missing from downstairs, none of which was found in the search of the house, or reported by the capital's pawnbrokers. But found or not, the meagreness of the haul was problematic. Thefts in Mayfair were usually much more substantial. Inspector Beresford had recently solved a spectacular case when he apprehended "a Spaniard of dwarf stature, and very fashionably dressed" who had stolen more than £4,500 worth of valuables from his master while they were staying at the Clarendon Hotel on New Bond Street. Guessing that the suspect would try to leave the country as quickly as possible, Beresford made an immediate search of the Steam Packet Wharf at London Bridge, spotted the dwarf on the deck of the *City of Boulogne* and gave chase. The stolen emerald pin which the thief was sporting in his cravat was said to be worth £50 alone. Lord William's rings, by comparison, would only have fetched a few guineas, and Mary Hannell's silver thimble a shilling if you were lucky.

There was growing interest in the presence of the book and spectacles in the victim's bedroom: was it relevant that Sir Samuel Romilly, the subject of the book, and Lord William's friend, had also died from having his throat slit—even though he was known to have been a suicide? The condition and position of the lights in the bedroom were also raising questions, for several people, including Mr. William Russell, Sarah Mancer and James Ellis (whom Mr. Russell had called in as a trustworthy assistant), asserted categorically that

Lord William *never* read in bed. And even if he had for once changed this habit of a lifetime, why would he have placed the candle so far away? The rushlight had not burned out, as one would have expected; Beresford conducted some experiments and concluded that it had been extinguished after about an hour and a half, that is, at approximately one in the morning. That, they deduced, must have been the time of the murder.

Beresford also tested Louisa Anstruther's evidence by sending his colleague Inspector Nicholas Pearce round to her bedroom at number 13 and carrying out a groan experiment at varying volumes, concluding that any sound from Lord William's side of the wall would have had to be quite loud to be heard at all. Much of the new evidence coming forward seemed to complicate rather than help solve the case: one of Mr. Loyd's maids thought she had seen a light on in the lumber room of number 14 on the evening of the murder, where there had never been a light before. But it was a locked room, and the key was kept in the maid and cook's bedroom next door, both of whom denied having set foot in the place for months. Now it was searched as thoroughly as the kitchen, pantry and outbuildings, for if any of the servants had been involved in the crime, some missing items would have to have been hidden on the premises. Finding them became the new focus of the investigation.

Sarah Mancer, who was a forthright young woman with no particular fondness for the new valet, had begun to tell the police in detail about some of their recent conversations. On the afternoon of the murder, when Courvoisier's mistake over the carriage was revealed, she remembered that he had said, "I shall tell [Lord William] I understood him to say half past five." When the maid advised he shouldn't lie to cover up his own mistake, Courvoisier replied that Lord William was always forgetting things "and ought to pay for his forgetfulness." And later that evening, when they had taken supper together and were talking about the change of cook, Courvoisier had said that if his Lordship didn't take the person he had recommended as her replacement, he wouldn't bother making any further suggestions. "He said he wished he had not come into his Lordship's service—he did not like him, he was too fidgety." When they had been in Richmond at Easter, Courvoisier complained, the fuss over everything had been extraordinary: Lord William had demanded three changes of room at the Castle Hotel, and fretted continually about the loss of his locket. It was insulting to be accused of theft from an employer, and Courvoisier felt he kept getting the blame for things he had not done.

Behind the scenes, the police had been moving swiftly to find Henry Carr. He had been called as a witness at the inquest, so his non-appearance naturally alarmed them, and as soon as Courvoisier mentioned the Royal Exchange public house, Superintendent Baker sent a group of constables over there to surround the building and watch for the suspect. Business was busy and noisy that night at the pub; this is where the raffle for his gun was going on, but Carr was nowhere to be seen (though quite how the police expected to recognize him is unclear: perhaps they questioned all young men of his general description). It took until three in the morning for the police, led by Beresford, to track Carr down to a room in a lodging house on North Terrace off South Street, five minutes' walk from Lord William's house. There had been no previous intimation that he was living so very near the scene of the crime; Courvoisier had made him sound like a visitor from out of town, not a neighbour.

The Times the next day said that Carr had been "closely questioned" by Beresford in the middle of the night and a statement extracted from him. He claimed that on the night of the murder he had gone back to his lodgings at around 10:30 and let himself in with a latch-key, not disturbing any of the other inhabitants, and that during the evening just passed, he'd been at the Royal Exchange between 9 and 11, at the raffle. Although the account he gave of his movements was "not perfectly satisfactory," and although neither the landlady of the Exchange nor any customers could say they'd seen him, there wasn't enough here for the police to make an arrest and they had to let Carr remain in his four-shilling room unmolested.

Whoever the murderer was, he or she had failed to anticipate how animated the Metropolitan Police could be with the commissioners breathing down their necks, and the government pressuring the commissioners in turn over a matter related so closely to a powerful Cabinet minister and of interest to the monarch herself. Much to everyone's surprise, the new consort, Prince Albert, was sending frequent messages to the house to enquire how the investigation was going. The Duke of Wellington, more tetchily, also wrote to the police commissioners, telling them to hurry up and solve the case. It was causing too much disturbance. The grand old soldier's instincts were undoubtedly correct: a form of panic, "almost unprecedented," was spreading among many of the wealthier residents of Mayfair, "and the feeling of apprehension for personal safety increases every hour." Lord Charles Greville, a stalwart of the glamorous Gore House set, got back from Newmarket during the week to find everyone obsessed by the murder, "which has excited a prodigious interest and frightened all London out of its wits. Visionary servants and air-drawn razors or carving knives dance before everybody's imagination, and half the world go to sleep expecting to have their throats cut before morning."

William Thackeray was inclined to be satirical about the class anxieties that the murder had brought to the surface, and told his mother that he had the perfect self-defence plan, which was "to murder old John [his manservant] and rob him of his money," for no one could be as badly off as himself. But few residents of Mayfair were inclined to be so flippant. The thought that one was not safe, even in this most exclusive neighbourhood, and that the servants with whom one shared a home might be turning on their masters, fitted all too well with the prevailing sense of threat from the lower orders. Could this be the beginnings of the uprising which the recent riots and demonstrations threatened?

Norfolk Street became a site of ghoulish tourism, and the first Sunday after the crime proved a particularly busy day after the *Sunday Times* published a set of sketches purporting to show the maid discovering the robbery, the valet and the maid finding the gashed body, and two top-hatted policemen "searching the jewel case." Some observers stopped just long enough to have a look up at the second-floor windows; others stayed for hours, gossiping. A sharp shower of rain dispersed the crowd at around 5 p.m., but as soon as it was over, they started to filter back. A poem that appeared in the *Metropolitan Magazine*, written by a Mrs. Abdy, "Lines on the Death of Lord William Russell: written after passing his residence on Norfolk Street, on Saturday, May 9th," moves from the sight of the crowds outside the house to imagining the scene within, where "remorseless hands have torn/ His spirit from its calm abode":

Yet no—the crowds who hover near
A tale of dreadful import breathe;
How shrinks the startled sense to hear
Of violent and ruthless death!

Yet one gets the impression Mrs. Abdy was relishing the horror as much as anyone, and was keenly interested in the onlookers' speculations:

Some sigh and shudder while they speak,
Mourning that guilt so dark should be,
And some, with wild conjectures, seek
To pierce the veil of mystery.

Yet let us not too rashly yield
To vague surmises on the crime:
The murderer's name shall stand revealed,
Doubtless, in God's appointed time.

That appointed time drew nearer as pressure grew on the police to establish a strong lead or come up with some relevant evidence. They interviewed Lord William's past servants, the neighbours, the tradesmen; they pondered why the dog had been removed to the stables (he always was) and whether a pillow could have been used to staunch the blood from the victim's throat. Mary Hannell now remembered that, as well as the beer, Courvoisier had offered them some sweet heavy wine on Tuesday night from a small bottle, "the same, he said, as his master had had at a party"; a growing suspicion that the female servants might have been drugged, and that drugs might have been used to sedate Lord William, led to further disturbance of the corpse in a post-mortem examination on Sunday 10 May, conducted by Henry Elsgood and John Nussey. Nothing unusual, however, was found when they opened the body and tested the contents of the stomach.

Henry Carr's lodgings were searched, but no stolen goods or weapons were found there. He did, however, have an unusually large amount of cash in his desk—£21—the source of which he couldn't explain beyond it being part of his savings. Those savings turned out to be extraordinarily high (£80 in Fector's bank in Dover) for someone whose last job paid only twenty-five guineas a year; Carr had even been able to lend money to friends—including Courvoisier—though admitting that he had done "little or nothing" by way of work since April 1839. Keen to find out more about his unusual circumstances, the police cautioned Carr and conveyed him to Norfolk Street to be questioned further at the scene of the crime, where, rather surprisingly, John Minet Fector, his former employer (and Courvoisier's), attempted to see him, but was refused.

The police were being bombarded with letters from members of the public, offering their services as amateur sleuths or proffering suggestions as to where the murder weapon or stolen goods might be secreted: the water tanks, the mattresses, the lamp post outside the house, the rooks' nests in Hyde Park, perhaps even inside the victim's body itself. A bootmaker wrote to say that his daughter had dreamed that the murder weapon was hidden in a window box; had they searched the geraniums? An anonymous tip-off claimed that a man with a wooden leg had been trying to sell a watch seal in a pub off Belgrave Square; another note said that a man with his arm in a sling had been acting suspiciously at the inquest: were they in any way connected with the case?

But a breakthrough had come on Friday 8 May when the

sharp-eyed Inspector Pearce noticed that the skirting board
in the butler's pantry looked loose: they wrenched it off and
behind it discovered five of Lord William's rings and some
gold coins in a purse. The next skirting board concealed a
missing Waterloo medal and a £10 note. Small objects, carefully hidden. Pearce, hoping to shake the valet's strictly
maintained composure, asked Commissioner Mayne if he
could challenge Courvoisier with these discoveries, and was
given the go-ahead. "I suspected what he might say might
be evidence," Pearce said later, defending himself against the
charge of trying to extort a confession, "it might be for him
and it might be against him." When he confronted the suspect with the rings and the medal, however, and said, "I have
found these things concealed in your pantry: *can you now
look me in the face?*" the valet, affronted, denied all knowledge of the items, their theft or concealment, and said his
conscience was completely clear. Courvoisier had adopted a
similarly wounded tone earlier in the week when the police
searched his person and questioned his assertion that a small
locket they found on him, wrapped in brown paper, was his
own. "When I find that the truth has been spoken I will then
tell all I know about it," he told one of the officers, cryptically.

It was of course possible that someone other than the valet
had secreted the stolen items in his pantry, but the chain of
suspicion kept leading in the same direction. The search intensified, and when the pantry window was inspected closely,
some marks were found that suggested someone had climbed
in or out of it. The amount of money Courvoisier had on him
that week seemed suspicious for someone who had recently
claimed to have only £8 in the world and, under interroga-
tion, more and more of his conversations seemed suspicious
too. Sarah Mancer now remembered that Carr and Cour-

voisier had been talking about money on the afternoon of the murder: Courvoisier complained that he had been required to settle his tailor's bill (a large one) without having received any wages yet from this job; he thought he was probably worse off now than when he first arrived in England (which was something he'd also said to a servant in Richmond). And both Sarah and Mary Hannell had twice heard him say that if he had "old Billy's" money, he'd not stay long in this country.

When several more items—Lord William's watch, seals and another ring—were found hidden under the lead around the pantry sink and a locket beneath the hearthstone, the discovery was kept secret from Courvoisier, but the atmosphere in the house changed. The locket was shown to Sarah Mancer and to Lord William's former valet, James Ellis, who both confirmed that it was the very one Lord William thought he had lost at the Castle Hotel the month before, when only the valet and groom, a young man called George Doubleday, had been with him. The police decided that they had enough evidence now to make an arrest and at 11:30 on Sunday evening told Courvoisier—who had been allowed to go to bed—to get dressed again and prepare to leave the house. A carriage was readied just round the corner in Green Street, with the horses' heads pointing towards Park Street for the quickest getaway, then Courvoisier was bundled out between Baker and Pearce, with another inspector following behind, all in plain clothes, to evade curious eyes. They made off at speed for Bow Street police court, where the valet was taken into a private room and this entered on the charge sheet: "Francis Benjamin Courvoisier, charged with the wilful murder of Lord William Russell, on the 6th instant, at No.14, Norfolkstreet, Park-lane." He was to appear before the magistrate next morning, "a middle-sized man, rather stoutly made," as *The Times* reported, "and aged, we should suppose, about 30. The expression of his countenance is dull and heavy, and there is not much of a foreigner in his general appearance. He has a down look, and his face and lips were deadly pale."

With renewed energy, the police began to look into Courvoisier's background, his friends, his family back in Switzerland, his Mayfair haunts, searching for any clues to his circumstances and the workings of his mind. No one at this stage thought to enquire what he had been reading.

3

"This Nightmare of a Book"

IN THE SUMMER OF 1840, THE WHOLE OF LONDON, FROM monarch to maidservants, was gripped by the unfolding drama in Norfolk Street, but behind it lay another story, a work of fiction, and an ardent debate about the dangers of glamorizing vice and whether or not serious crime should be portrayed in fiction at all.

If, that year, anyone had walked into the circulating libraries on the Strand, or the bookshops along Piccadilly, or the gentlemen's clubs and reading rooms of Mayfair, and asked who was the most celebrated novelist of the day, he would have been as likely to hear the name of William Harrison Ainsworth as that of Edward Bulwer (later Bulwer-Lytton), Thomas Lister or Charles Dickens. Ainsworth was the golden boy of his generation, a charming and talented Manchester lawyer who had moved to the capital in the 1820s in pursuit of the literary life, becoming at various times a journalist, publisher, editor, poet, playwright and novelist. His literary heroes were Sir Walter Scott and Alexandre Dumas, and Scott's praise of his first novel, a historical romance called *Sir John Chiverton*, very much helped launch the young Mancunian's career. He found other influential supporters in Thomas Campbell, editor of the *New Monthly Magazine*,

Charles Lamb, the famous essayist, and John Ebers, editor of the *Literary Souvenir* and owner of the Opera House in the Haymarket, whose daughter, Fanny, Ainsworth married in 1826, at the age of twenty-one.

It helped that as well as being clever, original and "without a particle of conceit," Ainsworth was also dazzlingly good-looking. "You see what a pretty fellow THE young Novelist of the Season is," William Maginn wrote in *Fraser's Magazine* in 1834, opposite a specially commissioned portrait of the writer, "how exactly, in fact, he resembles one of the most classically handsome and brilliant of the established lady-killers." One of the best dressed too: the "dashing outline of back, hip, thigh, leg, etc., etc." that Maginn couldn't help noticing was set off in classic dandy fashion by beautifully tailored high-collared coats, tight trousers, jewelled pins, numerous rings and a seemingly endless supply of gorgeously patterned waistcoats.

Artistic and literary London in 1840 was an exclusive society, based around the salons of influential hostesses such as Lady Holland and Marguerite Power, the Countess of Blessington, wealthy writers such as Samuel Rogers and Richard Monckton Milnes (who was also an MP), and one or two gentlemen's clubs. Lady Holland's circle at Holland House was frequented by Whigs and liberals such as Lord Brougham, Lord Grey and the Russells, while the Countess, editor of two influential anthologies and a prolific writer of criticism and verse, attracted a rather more outré crowd at Gore House, owing to the scandalous nature of her relationship with her son-in-law, the dandy poet and painter Count Alfred d'Orsay.[*]

---

[*] After the Countess's husband, the Earl of Blessington, died in 1829, d'Orsay (who was married to the Countess's stepdaughter, Harriet) set up home with her, first at Seamore Place and later at Gore House.

Then there were the periodicals—Leigh Hunt's *Examiner*, the *Monthly Magazine, Blackwood's, Fraser's, Bentley's*, the *Athenaeum*, the *Spectator*, the *Quarterly*—each with its own distinctive slant on politics, literature and art, each with its own coterie and axes to grind. "Wars" between the magazines were entered into with frequency and conducted with relish in the spirit of intellectual sparring; but there were also sustained campaigns against particular authors and issues, which could do real damage. Ainsworth had been one of the original *Fraser's* group, but even he became a target for virulent attack from the magazine over his most controversial novel.

Ainsworth was fortunate to have come of age as a writer at exactly the moment when the market for books was expanding at previously unimaginable speed, fuelled by new, much cheaper printing methods and a rapidly growing readership among the literate working class; in the 1820s and 1830s, literacy was becoming, in effect, industrialized. Publishers such as Henry Colburn and Richard Bentley were making fortunes; old texts could be picked up for next to nothing and sold cheaply (as Bentley did with the works of the late Miss Jane Austen) while new works could be sold to the public several times over: as serials in magazines (with the story often spread out tantalizingly over twenty months or more), in separate paper-covered instalments, and finally in hardback, three-volume form. Prices of books had decreased sharply with mass production, and while, at over twenty shillings, it was still beyond most working men's means to buy a novel, new titles sold in their tens of thousands to the circulating libraries, where you could purchase a year's subscription for about the price of one book. Suddenly, the latest works of fiction were not just being discussed by the chattering classes in dining rooms, clubs and salons but, as the *Examiner* complained, "low smoking rooms, the common barbers' shops, the cheap reading places, the private booksellers', and the minor theatres."

The titles that went down spectacularly well with this new mass audience were, predictably, the most sensational ones, like Bulwer's *Paul Clifford* (a gripping outlaw tale, published in 1830[*]), Bulwer's fictionalized account of the real-life murderer Eugene Aram (1832), or Charles Whitehead's *Lives and Exploits of English Highwaymen, Pirates and Robbers* (1834). They spawned a whole school of criminal romance, known disparagingly as "Newgate novels" after the grisly catalogues of crime and punishment that inspired them in *The Newgate Calendar; or, Malefactors' Bloody Register* (first published in 1773)—violent, intriguing and thoroughly addictive true-life cases.

Robbers, murderers and thugs had of course been portrayed in literature many times before, but seldom promoted to the status of hero, nor written about by aristocratic types like Bulwer (a baronet, and on his way to becoming an earl) and discussed admiringly by lords and ladies at the top of the *ton*. Pierce Egan had led the way in the 1820s with his wildly successful *Life in London* sketches, the adventures of two young men-about-town called Tom and Jerry who move across the city and across social divides, finding numerous satiric parallels between high and low life. Egan's sparky stories made boozing dens and the rough-and-ready theatres known as "penny gaffs" seem a lot more vital than their middle- and upper-class counterparts, and created a vogue for the criminal-class slang called "flash cant," which the Newgate novelists revived energetically. This complex dialect

---

[*] *Paul Clifford* is the book that begins, "It was a dark and stormy night . . ."

(derived from Romany) added an authentic flavour to depic-
tions of low life, but also signalled sympathy with underclass
culture generally, putting it forward as an area of legitimate
interest.

Alongside his crimes, a Newgate hero typically keeps displaying strains of noble feeling: Paul Clifford sacrifices his
love for a spotless girl because he deems himself unworthy
of her (unlike his corrupt, but outwardly respectable, rival),
while Eugene Aram (in Bulwer's interpretation) is a positive
model of scholarly rectitude, yearning for "chances of illuminating mankind." It was the blurring of moral signals in these
books that alarmed the critics, who thought they gave birth
to something worse than bad taste: "We say, let your rogues in
novels act like rogues and your honest men like honest men,"
Fraser's urged. "Don't let us have any juggling and thimble-
rigging with virtue and vice, so that at the end of three volumes, the bewildered reader shall not know which is which."

But for working-class readers, there was suddenly a new
type of fiction which celebrated the native cunning, ambition
and potential of the ordinary man, and they loved it. Punishment catches up with a Newgate hero eventually, but only
as the curtain falls: his vitality is what impresses most. Paul
Clifford's preference for "the jolly, bold and free" life of a robber on the road, for instance, seems quite reasonable when
the alternative is poverty and want. And though Bulwer
never admitted to the subversive potential of his book, Paul
Clifford's career has definite Robin Hood appeal too, as all
his genteel victims are depicted, to a greater or lesser extent,
as species of robber themselves.

Ainsworth had kept a keen eye on Bulwer's and Whitehead's successes, and in 1834 produced a Newgate novel of
his own, a gothic thriller called *Rookwood*, set in the 1730s.

The plot revolves around hidden crimes within an ancient family, but the episodes which really fired up the public imagination were those connected with the highwayman Dick Turpin, and the thrilling "Ride to York" in which he outstrips his captors. Ainsworth made this so convincing that it was widely believed as fact, and innkeepers and ostlers along the Great North Road began claiming that Turpin had stopped to buy ale from their ancestors, or had refreshed his horse Black Bess at their troughs.

Bulwer boasted how he had interviewed professional thieves for *Paul Clifford* to master his smattering of "flash"; Ainsworth was equally keen to display his low-life credentials by inventing "a *purely flash* song" in *Rookwood*, called "Nix My Dolly," "[whose] great and peculiar merit consists in its being utterly incomprehensible to the uninformed understanding." This was a sly joke: Ainsworth guessed how attractively edgy his flash songs would appear to middle-class audiences (rather like rap today). His own acquisition of the language was purely synthetic; Ainsworth said that he got it all from reading the memoirs of an ex-convict, James Hardy Vaux, and knew no criminals personally. But his use of "the lingo" was so convincing that the reviewer in *Fraser's* quoted a former criminal as saying, "Are you quite *sure* that the writer of this book has never been one of the Family?"

Rookwood changed Ainsworth's fortunes overnight. "It is doing famously well here," he wrote to his Mancunian friend James Crossley in the first flush of his success, "making, in fact, quite a *sensation*. It has been praised in quarters of which you can have no idea . . . In fact, as Byron says, I went to bed unknown, arose, and found myself famous." Reprints came thick and fast, along with broadsheets and ballads pirating the story; stage versions, some very crude, popped up in theatres across the capital, and at Astley's Amphitheatre there was a spectacular representation of "Turpin's Ride," featuring real horses. Most impressive of all, in what must have been the first such publicity campaign for an author, Ainsworth's portrait was pasted up in many of London's brand-new horse-drawn omnibuses, where it was "eagerly examined and discussed" by passengers.

Rookwood was also Ainsworth's ticket of admission to the Gore House set, where the Countess of Blessington was as delighted with the novelist's looks as with his books. Was he not the double of d'Orsay? she asked, as she placed herself between them by the fireplace one evening, saying she had the two handsomest men in London for her supporters. Ainsworth was grateful for the chance to reinvent himself as a sought-after celebrity, for his private life was in disarray. His marriage failed in the year of *Rookwood*, and he left home (and three young daughters) to go and live with his cousin's widow, Eliza Buckley, and her sister Anne in a house in Kensal Green, then a bosky hamlet well outside town. Eliza was a handsome, highly intelligent woman of forty-seven, who held emphatic opinions and expressed them freely (her married name, Mrs. Touchet, seems singularly appropriate), and though Ainsworth behaved like the head of the household at Kensal Lodge, entertaining his friends lavishly there, everyone noticed how much influence Mrs. T. had over him, and it seems highly likely that their relationship was somewhat more than cousinly.

It was around the time of his move to Kensal Lodge that Ainsworth met and befriended a 24-year-old parliamentary reporter called Charles Dickens, as yet unpublished, unmarried and decidedly unfamous. Dickens admired Ainsworth exceedingly at this date—essentially, he wanted to *be* him, to have his astonishing good looks, his easy-going nature, his bachelor lifestyle, his ecstatic fans. In emulation of the d'Orsay-Ainsworth group, young Dickens spent much more on clothes than he could strictly afford, and was described by one onlooker in the 1830s as wearing "a swallow-tail coat with a very high velvet collar; a voluminous satin stock with a double breast-pin; a crimson velvet waistcoat over which meandered a lengthy gold chain."

Ainsworth introduced Dickens to a wide circle of highly influential people, including Dickens's future illustrator George Cruikshank, and future biographer John Forster, a brilliant, acerbic young lawyer from Newcastle, who was already known as one of the *Examiner*'s spikiest critics. Together, Ainsworth, Dickens and Forster formed the "Trio Club," and were, for a short time, inseparable friends, travelling around the country together, taking long walks and rides, going to the theatre (to which Dickens was even more addicted than Ainsworth), or throwing down their gloves at Gore House, and talking all the time of books and business.

Ainsworth also introduced Dickens to John Macrone, and encouraged the publisher to bring out some of Dickens's journalism as a book (published in 1836 as *Sketches by Boz*). Among the new pieces Dickens wrote for his debut was "A Visit to Newgate," a vivid account of the prison and its inmates, including a highly imaginative description of a condemned man's last night (which he worked into *Oliver Twist* later). In a room that opened on to the street of the Old Bailey Dickens had been shown a collection of leg irons, "including those worn by the redoubtable Jack Sheppard—genuine; and those *said* to have been graced by the limbs of the no less celebrated Dick Turpin—doubtful." It was Ainsworth who had been talking to him about the eighteenth century thief,

Jack Sheppard (a subject he had in mind for a future book), and who had told him that the Turpin relics at Newgate were apocryphal. The younger writer needed no more excuse to slip in a fulsome tribute to his friend, saying "after the ride [Mr. Ainsworth] has given us in company with that renowned hero, we will implicitly believe anything he may please to write about him."

Dickens was already planning a novel of his own which would develop several of the themes in "A Visit to Newgate," to be called *Gabriel Vardon, the Locksmith of London*, set during the period of the anti-Catholic Gordon Riots in the 1780s. But while *Sketches by Boz* was being prepared for the press, he was diverted by a request to write some stories to accompany a set of sporting prints. The result was *The Posthumous Papers of the Pickwick Club*, the first and least typical of all the great novels which were to flow subsequently from Dickens's pen.

The year 1836 was an incredibly busy and successful one for the young writer. *Pickwick* took off spectacularly and put him in high demand, prompting Richard Bentley to move in quickly with a contract for two more novels and the editorship of a new monthly magazine, *Bentley's Miscellany*, which would feature fiction serials. Dickens also got married that year, to Catherine Hogarth (always called "Kate" by him), and soon she was pregnant with the first of their ten children. The punishing work ethic that he kept to all his life became well established, and by the time the first issue of *Bentley's Miscellany* went to press, in January 1837, he had the first few instalments ready of a new novel in twenty parts.

Oliver Twist was not quite what fans of *Pickwick* were expecting to see next and was immediately classed with the Newgate school. In fact it rather out-Newgated Bulwer's and

Ainsworth's works with its sympathetic portrait of London's pickpockets and thieves and the gruesome account of Bill Sikes's murder of Nancy. Brilliant creations such as the Artful Dodger, with his mastery of flash, and Fagin (based on a notorious real-life fence called Ikey Solomons, who had been transported to Australia in 1830) captivated the public, and the book sold copiously in both official and pirated forms, taking "felon literature" into ever wider social circles. The new monarch, Queen Victoria, found the story "excessively interesting," young Lord William Russell recommended it warmly to his wife, and Edwin Landseer loved the book so much that he insisted on reading parts of it aloud to his students at the Royal Academy during life classes. Landseer's father, John, however, dismissed the book as "some of Dickens's nonsense"; like many commentators in the press, he thought Newgate novels went much too far in glamorizing vice. Elsewhere there was disquiet at the explicit violence in the story, particularly the murder of Nancy, of which Richard Horne (a friend of Dickens) wrote, "a more ferocious and ghastly deed was never perpetrated."

Dickens's friendship with Ainsworth deepened in these two years; they were sharing ideas freely and even planning a collaboration, "to illustrate ancient and modern London in a Pickwick form." Ainsworth craved more of the *Rookwood* effect and knew how to get it. "The truth is, to write for the mob, we must not write too well," he told Crossley. "The newspaper level is the true line to take. In proportion as Dickens departs from this, he will decline in popular favour—of this I am certain. I think, however, he has so much tact that he will yet retrieve himself—and become bad enough to suit all tastes."

But Dickens was rapidly finding his own way to a mass

audience, and did not need this dubious advice. While *Oliver Twist* was still being serialized and *Gabriel Vardon* ticked along slowly, he had begun *Nicholas Nickleby*, a novel much more about contemporary social evils than crime. It was Ainsworth who studied to cultivate "the newspaper level" with his choice of another real-life blackguard as his next subject, and it was Ainsworth who fell foul of the critics for wanting to appeal to "the mob" at all.

Jack Sheppard's history was a staple of *The Newgate Calendar*, and well known all through the eighteenth century. Born in 1702, his short career as a petty thief was unexceptional but he became famous for evading capture and making a series of spectacular, seemingly impossible, prison breaks. Sheppard had escaped through the ceiling of St. Giles's Roundhouse, by bedsheet from Clerkenwell Prison, dressed as a woman from Newgate, and then, when consigned to Newgate's infamous dungeon, the Castle, and manacled to the floor, he managed to pick the locks of his irons with a small nail, climb the chimney, penetrate several more locked doors and escape from the roof via another improvised rope. Getting rearrested soon after, and then hanged, did little to detract from the glamour of these apparent superpowers.

Daniel Defoe, Sheppard's contemporary, had written about him, and about his nemesis, the "thief-catcher" Jonathan Wild; Sheppard was also the model for John Gay's Macheath in *The Beggar's Opera* and for Hogarth's "Idle Apprentice" in his great series of prints, *Industry and Idleness*, much reproduced in the century since Sheppard's death. Ainsworth saw the potential in the old story, highlighted the escape-artistry, played down the crimes, inserted several subplots about hidden parentage and lost estates, and introduced a devoted criminal friend and a saintly, destitute mother. It was a promising formula.

Ainsworth's version of the story starts in 1703 with the adoption of the infant Jack by a respectable carpenter called Owen Wood, who braves entering a criminal ghetto south of the river to fetch him. "The Mint" is beyond the reach of the law and its inhabitants look out for each other with brutal efficiency: when a fugitive aristocrat and a second baby appear at Jack's mother's house, his pursuers are in turn being pursued by a mob of the locals, alerted to the invasion of their turf. These are almost the only scenes in which "flash" is used extensively, but the effect, sudden and overwhelming, is of being transported to another world altogether.

> "Ay, ay, it's all bob, my covey! You're safe enough, that's certain!" responded the Minters, baying, yelping, leaping and howling around him like a pack of hounds . . . "but, where are the lurchers?"
> "Who?" asked Wood.
> "The traps!" responded a bystander.
> "The shoulder-clappers!"

And within just a few pages there is not only this plunge into an alien language and culture, but riotous violence, a pursuit across rooftops and a high-octane description of a storm on the Thames at night.

The fugitive aristocrat drowns in the storm, leaving Wood with two babies to look after, and the second part of the book moves us along twelve years to show how these two boys' lives have diverged: Thames (named after the river) is upright and incorruptible and reads patriotic ballads and books about geometry, but Jack is already a casual thief, and addicted to "those Froissarts and Holinsheds of crime—the Ordinaries of Newgate" (*The Newgate Calendar*) and "flash songs." The effects of his literary diet are already obvious in Jack's light-fingeredness, and the use of his carpentry skills not to finish work for his father but to make himself a toy gallows. Bulwer's Paul Clifford was also shown to have turned to a life of crime after reading *The Newgate Calendar*, and, in Dickens's story, Fagin gives a copy of the book to Oliver Twist. It's strange that the very novels that came to represent all that was bad about this type of reading matter contain such specific warnings against it.

Jack carves his name on a beam in the workshop to mimic "great men" such as the highwayman Claude Duval who had carved their names on the stones of Newgate. A life of crime might be worth the possible punishment, Jack reckons, "if my name should become as famous as theirs." This image, memorably captured by George Cruikshank in his illustrations, became the one used on posters all over town to advertise both the book and the play: a quasi-religious tableau of a young man, standing on a bench to reach the beam, glimpsing his way to glory. Soon we see Jack (still aged only about twelve) utterly acclimatized to the life of a petty criminal, lounging in the Cross Shovels—a "flash ken"—smoking, drinking and being pawed by two prostitutes, Edgeworth Bess and Poll Maggot. Housebreaking is his new hobby, and nihilism his creed: "Nobody's disgraced and ruined unless he's found out," the youth tells his horrified brother.

Jack gets caught up in the criminal underworld dominated by Jonathan Wild, a ruthless blackmailer and extortionist who also happened to be a law enforcer, and in its later chap-

ters the book becomes increasingly violent, with a ghastly
scene in which Wild bludgeons Sir Rowland Trenchard and
throws him down a well to die, and another, worse, scene in
which Wild's psychopathic sidekick Blueskin is subjected to
peine forte et dure (by which a prisoner was slowly crushed
with increasing weights). The lengthy description of this tor-
ture seems a gratuitous indulgence on Ainsworth's part and
also incredible, as Blueskin survives it in sufficient health to
escape and take revenge on Wild by slitting his throat.

But the scene which caused most concern later, and which
was taken by some as the blueprint for the crime in Norfolk
Street, was the one in which Ainsworth describes in detail
how Jack and Blueskin go about burgling the Woods' house
in Dollis Hill, bringing some meat to quieten the guard dog,
taking off their boots and "treading upon the point of their
toes so cautiously, that not a board creaked beneath their
weight."* In the bedroom, Jack forces a bureau while Blueskin pulls the plate chest out from under the bed. Everything
seems to be going well for the robbers until Jack leaves Blueskin alone in the Woods' room while he goes off to steal their
daughter's valuables, and Mrs. Wood, waking and raising the
alarm, struggles to wrest the sack of swag from the intruder:

> "Leave go!" thundered Blueskin—"leave go—you'd
> better!"—and he held the sack as firmly as he could
> with one hand, while with the other he searched for
> his knife.
>   "No, I won't leave go!" screamed Mrs. Wood.
> "Fire!—murder!—thieves!—I've got one of 'em!"

---

* Cruikshank's illustration of the scene shows two masked intruders, one
carrying a bludgeon and one a knife, standing over the sleeping couple.

"Come along," cried Jack.

"I can't," answered Blueskin. "This she-devil has got hold of the sack. Leave go, I tell you!" and he forced open the knife with his teeth.

"Help!—murder!—thieves!" screamed Mrs. Wood;— "Owen!—Owen!—Thames!—help!"

"Coming!" cried Mr. Wood, leaping from the bed. "Where are you?"

"Here," replied Mrs. Wood. "Help—I'll hold him!"

"Leave her," cried Jack, darting down-stairs, amid a furious ringing of bells,—"the house is alarmed,— follow me!"

"Curses light on you!" cried Blueskin, savagely; "since you won't be advised, take your fate."

And seizing her by the hair, he pulled back her head, and drew the knife with all his force across her throat. There was a dreadful stifled groan, and she fell heavily upon the landing.

In January 1839, with his new novel well under way, Ainsworth took Dickens on a festive trip to Manchester to attend a public dinner in their honour, with Forster in tow. It wasn't quite Dickens's first visit: he and the artist Hablot Browne and Forster had been up a few months before on a research trip, when one breakfast guest had been struck by how effeminate "Boz" looked, with his long hair and shiny boots. They had also on that occasion been out to visit Ainsworth's three daughters at school in Cheadle, but one of the girls thought Forster was a dentist, and burst into tears.

The proud civic dinner in his native city was one of the most gratifying incidents in Ainsworth's career, according to his biographer, S. M. Ellis, but there was some confusion—never resolved—over who exactly was guest of honour. Ainsworth had naturally assumed it was himself (since the initial invitation was addressed to him), but as the date drew nearer the city authorities harped so much on "Boz's" presence that some doubt appeared, and the friends ended up treating it as a joint festival, receiving all the toasts and bumpers as a sort of celebrity double-act.

The trip to Manchester, with its cheerful round of dinners and speeches, showed Ainsworth and Dickens in a state of balance, but the younger writer was about to pull ahead. Dickens was feeling his power: though Bentley had increased his promised payments for the Gordon Riots novel (now called *Barnaby Rudge*) from £200 to a massive £4,000,* he wanted the book finished much sooner than Dickens was prepared to oblige, and the writer, no longer desperate for money, promptly resigned from the editorship of the *Miscellany*. Forster was deeply implicated in all this, egging Dickens on to defy Bentley, complaining to the publisher on Dickens's behalf and writing emotional letters to Ainsworth about the dangers of Bentley's "fetters." Ainsworth dismissed Forster's warnings, and was happy to take over the editorship of *Bentley's Miscellany* that spring: for one thing, he *did* need the money, and Forster's partisanship had a somewhat hysterical flavour. But he had no idea how personally Forster could feel such slights, nor how damaging an enemy his erstwhile Trio Club friend might become.

---

* Dickens's salary at the *Morning Chronicle* in 1834, when he got his first full-time job there, was 260 guineas a year, i.e., about fifteen times less than this payout from Bentley.

So Ainsworth was in charge of the magazine as the gripping last episodes of *Oliver Twist* appeared in its pages and the first instalments of his own *Jack Sheppard* were published alongside them, embellished with Cruikshank's arresting pictures. "I trust [it] will be as popular as thrice-lucky *Rookwood*," Ainsworth wrote to Crossley, cheered by some praising early notices and very lively sales. He did all he could to promote the book, suggesting the anniversary of Sheppard's execution on 16 November as the publication date for the three-volume edition (possibly the earliest instance of a publicity tie-in), which his friend Richard Harris Barham felt "should not be lost sight of in the *advertisement*."

Stage versions of novels were notoriously rough and ready in the days before efficient copyright law, and authors had very little influence over the use made of their work. Dickens had had to endure some appalling travesties, including a version of *Oliver Twist* at the Surrey in 1838 that was so bad he lay down in the box to avoid seeing too much of it. Authors weren't paid for the use of their texts, either, so had to be phlegmatic and hope the publicity was worthwhile. This was certainly how Ainsworth treated the craze for reproducing and pirating *Jack Sheppard* in the winter of 1839—to begin with, at any rate. Only a few days before a production opened at the Victoria in late October, Ainsworth, accompanied by Barham, went to give the dramatist William Moncrieff exclusive access to the story's denouement, which hadn't yet been published. But Moncrieff turned out to have little need of Ainsworth's help, jumping up and performing a rapid solo run-through of his planned production, "without having occasion to refer to any book or person." He had already settled on his own ending, though the novelist promised to send the official one along anyway.

Witnessing this must have brought home to Ainsworth his book's potential popularity. Tourists were already trying to find the "Cage" at Willesden from which Jack had escaped (made up by Ainsworth), and (ditto) Jack's mother's grave upon which so many filial tears had been shed; as with *Rookwood*, the novelist had managed to convince many readers that his inventions were true. Even in the early months of the serialization there were signs of "infatuation" among fans, which only grew as Jack's character became ever more noble, as it did, with suspicious purposefulness, about halfway through the book. Ainsworth was falling in love with his hero, but was he also reacting to the public's reception of the early chapters, and giving them more of what they wanted as he went along?

Ainsworth was criticized roundly for colluding with his publisher in the vulgar selling of a vulgar story, but his desire to put his imprimatur on *Jack Sheppard*, almost to trademark his interest in it, was understandable given the money to be made. It ended up doing him far more harm than good, though. By the end of the winter, *Jack Sheppard* had grown to a hydra-headed, extra-literary phenomenon, and just as Ainsworth at first got all the credit for it, later he had to take all the blame. He had no control over the crude knock-offs and plagiarisms of his novel that sprang up instantly, such as the chapbook versions (ingenious "digested reads" for those who couldn't afford to buy, or couldn't be bothered to read, the complete story). And no one who picked up a cheap "penny dreadful" on the street, or a suspiciously concise and ill-printed version of "Jack Sheppard, the daring housebreaker" at one of the print shops in Seven Dials, or who read, in the *Sunday Times*, a serial by "M. H. Ainsforth," would necessarily know or care who the author might be, or think about the text as anyone's intellectual property.

Lord William Russell's murderer was one such reader, and would have probably been unable to name the author of *Jack Sheppard*, except, in the depths of remorse, to think of that author as Satan. It was the *story* he consumed that winter, avidly and uncritically, in whichever version it was that fell into his hands. No debating the rights and wrongs of "felon literature," no qualms about "thimble-rigging with virtue and vice"; what he wanted, and got, was a riveting read about thieves and murderers that was lifelike and compelling. "Being under the dominion of Satan (I read it with pleasure), I did not think it would be a great sin to place myself among them. On the contrary, I admired their skill and their valour," this impressionable reader wrote in his own real-life Newgate narrative. "I was particularly struck with the history of a young man who was born of very respectable parents, and who had spent his property in gaming and debauchery, and afterwards went from place to place stealing all he could. I admired his cunning, instead of being horrified at it; and now I reap but two [*sic*] well the fruit of those papers and books."

While the public lapped up the story of the lovable thief during its serialization in 1839, the critics were sharpening their knives. "*Jack Sheppard* is a bad book, and what is worse, it is one of a class of bad books, got up for a bad public," the *Athenaeum* intoned portentously, "a melo-dramatic story of motiveless crime and impossible folly." The *Examiner* (Leigh Hunt's magazine) gave the novel an excoriating review, calling it "pernicious" and "poisonous," while in Philadelphia, the lead writer of *Graham's Magazine*, a young journalist called Edgar Allan Poe, who was about to publish his own first collection of stories, *Tales of the Grotesque and Arabesque*, damned the book outright: "[The author of *Jack Sheppard*] puts us out of all patience," he said. "His marvels have a nakedness which repels. Nothing he relates seems either probable or possible, or of the slightest interest. His hero impresses us as the merest chimera, with whom we have no earthly concern, and when he makes his final escape and comes to the gallows, we would feel a very sensible relief, but for the impracticality of hanging up Mr. Ainsworth in his stead."

But the most stinging review was that penned by Ainsworth's erstwhile friend John Forster, who seems to have forgotten that he had been cheering the author on before publication and had celebrated "little Jack Sheppard's christening dinner" the previous New Year at Kensal Lodge. "We notice this 'romance' with very great reluctance," he began, "because we have thought the author capable of better things. It is however in every sense of the word so bad, and has been recommended to circulation by such disreputable means that the silence we intended to preserve upon the subject would be almost as great a compromise with truth as the morals of the book or the puffs of the bookseller." How Ainsworth must have blanched when he read this—not least at Forster's shameless moralizing.

William Makepeace Thackeray watched the onslaught on *Jack Sheppard* with some complacency, since he had been attacking the Newgate novelists in print for the past six or seven years. Still in his twenties, and known mainly as an artist (he had been considered, but turned down, as illustrator both for Dickens's *Pickwick Papers* and Ainsworth's *Crichton*, the successor to *Rookwood*), Thackeray was struggling to make a living in any way he could, having inherited money from his father aged twenty-one, and then lost it all through gambling and a bank failure. By the late 1830s, this tall, burly, leonine young man, with a broken nose and rather dishevelled appearance, had a wife and two daughters to support and had taken on so much work at *Fraser's*, the *Morning Chronicle* and the *Foreign Quarterly Review* that readers might well have objected to a monopoly, had the author's own name not always been hidden by an ingenious multiplicity of aliases.

From behind these disguises, Thackeray carried on a vigorous campaign against the Newgate novels, which seemed to him essentially fraudulent, romanticizing atrocious crimes in "absurd and unreal" ways and written by men who had no actual knowledge of the thieves and cut-throats they seemed so fond of describing. The public's moral weakness was exploited by such literature, he argued, but, worse, the public seemed to prefer things that way: "We are sick of heroic griefs, passions, tragedies; but take them out of the palace, and place them in the thief's boozing ken—be prodigal of irony, of slang, and bad grammar—sprinkle with cant phrases—leave out the h's, double the v's, divide the w's (as may be necessary), and tragedy becomes interesting once more."

In a bold and bad move to counteract the trend (and perhaps make some money, too), Thackeray had decided to write a Newgate story of his own that would deliberately disgust readers, in order to produce "a wholesome nausea . . . and a more healthy habit." Writing under the pseudonym of Ikey Solomon Junior (a deliberate reference to Dickens's source for *Oliver Twist*), he chose the worst case history he could find in *The Newgate Calendar*, that of Catherine Hayes, who in 1726 had conspired with two men, one her lodger (and lover), the other reportedly her illegitimate son, to murder her husband, a London carpenter. The three got their victim drunk and then murdered him with a hatchet, chopping the body into many parts and disposing of it in different locations, the head being thrown into the Thames.

Thackeray had never written a novel before, but it's hard to see *Catherine* (published in instalments between May 1839 and February 1840) as the beginning of a career leading to the brilliance of *Vanity Fair* only eight years later. Having chosen such a repellent tale, he struggled to keep control of the tone, book-ending the crime with a heavily satirical prologue and a sombre, sermon-like postscript, both of which were guaranteed to bemuse readers rather than chasten them. And to keep to his scheme, he felt obliged to include a description of the crime itself, which was so brutal and explicit that it was censored from later Victorian editions, on the grounds that it had "no literary merit whatever" and was "simply horrible," a dreadful irony that Thackeray would have torn his hair to know of.

In later years, Thackeray understood the failure of *Catherine* and never sought to publish it in book form (that only happened after his death), but at the time he was prepared to risk a lot for this elaborate piece of propaganda. In his postscript he launched a full-scale attack on Dickens and the other Newgate novelists for abusing their own powers. Dickens's sympathetic criminals had stoked a public hunger, he said, "and so Jack Sheppard makes his appearance. Jack and his two wives, and his faithful Blueskin, and his gin-drinking mother, that sweet Magdalen! . . . We are taught to hate Wild, to be sure; but then it is because he betrays thieves, the rogue! And yet bad, ludicrous, monstrous as the idea of this book is, we read, and read, and are interested, too." And worse, once such novels were put on stage, in the crude forms which were so hugely popular and profitable, they became even more dangerous: "the whole London public, from peers to chimney-sweeps, are interested about a set of ruffians whose occupations are thievery, murder and prostitution."

Not all the literary satires on "the Jack Sheppard school," as it was now called, were as ponderous as *Catherine*. Theodore Hook (under the pseudonym of Bon Gaultier) played on the word "faking" (flash for "theft") to mock the class slumming that he felt Ainsworth, Bulwer and Dickens had indulged in:

> Come, all ye jolly covies, vot faking do admire,
> And pledge them British authors who to our line
>   aspire;
> Who, if they were not gemmen born, like us had
>   kicked at trade,
> And every von had turned him out a genuine fancy
>   blade . . .
>
> 'Tis them's the boys as knows the vorld, 'tis them as
>   knows mankind,
> And vould have picked his pocket too, if Fortune (vot
>   is blind)
> Had not, to spite their genius, stuck them in a false
>   position,
> Vere they can only write about, not execute their
>   mission . . .

And a very funny satire by John Poole appeared in the *New Monthly Magazine* for January 1840, in which Dick Swiveller tells his sidekick Nimble Joey how the Newgate stories smoothed his path to a life of crime: "All my larnin' I got by readin' books vot tells you how to do the trick, with picturs vot shows you the vay." In the theatres, too, Dick says:

> "The Surrey, and the Cobug, and the 'Delphi—one does pick up a bit at them 'ere places, blow me if one don't. Ah!" (added he with a sigh) "I vish I vas old enough to be a dashing *Scrog Swoggy*. That's *summat* like—*that's* your lark—*that's* the vay to be famous—*that's* the vay to get all the gals admirin' on you, and to get yourself 'mortalized and acted in a theatre . . . and if I don't live to 'stinguish myself more nor that—if I don't live to *squizzle* a *winny* as well as the best on 'em—"
>
> "Squizzle a winny!" echoed the squeamish novice; "cut a throat! I'm not ashamed to say, captain, I do almost think that I'm half-inclined to fancy I *should* feel a *leetle* objection to that."
>
> "Cut a throat, spoony? Who talked o' cutting a throat? Squizzle a winny, *I* said . . . it don't *sound* so awful-like, no, not in the least; and that makes the thoughts on it come not quite so unpleasant to one's mind."

But getting the readers of the *Monthly Magazine* to laugh themselves silly over this, as Richard Harris Barham did, and feel that the last word had been said in retort to the *Jack Sheppard* phenomenon just about guaranteed that it would burgeon beyond their notice. The book was attacked in the press, the courts and even the House of Commons, but the issues it stirred up could not be contained, or policed, by the usual moral guardians. Thackeray was sobered by the difference in circulation of James Catnatch's popular ballad collections and that of the literary press, hundreds of thousands to mere thousands, meaning that voices such as his, Forster's or even Ainsworth's were beginning to seem insignificant.

He was one of the only commentators to recognize that the stage versions of *Jack Sheppard* would take the story's audience to a whole new level, for it was only when the dramatizations opened—in a mad flurry towards the end of 1839—that the moral panic really began. The week that *Jack Sheppard* appeared as a three-volume novel, it also went on stage at the Surrey and the Queen's, followed rapidly by six other productions across the capital, at the Adelphi, Sadler's Wells, the Victoria, the City of London, the Garrick, the Pavilion and a pantomime version, *Harlequin Sheppard*, at Drury Lane around Christmastime. Suddenly, you could hardly move for the story of the defiant housebreaker, or miss the posters and playbills depicting his calling to crime.

But this was also the season in which the worst Chartist riot to date had taken place, in Newport, Monmouthshire, where a stand-off at the town hall on 4 November led to fourteen protesters being killed, and it was impossible for the press—and politicians, and magistrates—not to make connections between this alarming outburst of public unrest and the equally uncontrollable popularity of *Jack Sheppard*, with its "gross and violent excitements." The sudden success of such a vulgar play seemed symptomatic of what the *Monthly Review* called "those changes and intensities that mark our social condition and divisions,—to the strong growth, of the materiality and mechanical structure, so to speak, of the prevailing ideas and sympathies." And Jack as a representative ordinary underclass youth, launching out on a career of devil-may-care freedom, seemed an almost irresistibly attractive model to the disquieted lower orders, or "the Great Unwashed" as Bulwer had called them in *Paul Clifford*, who had begun to weigh heavily on the public consciousness.

The novel had also roused up a lot of latent anxiety among the chattering classes. From her sickbed in Torquay, where she had gone to spend the winter, the young poet Elizabeth Barrett's letters to her friend Mary Russell Mitford were much taken up with the *Jack Sheppard* controversy. Barrett wondered whether it was right to infer an author's morals from those of his or her fictional creations. "Sins of coarseness and affectation and latitudinarianism" had been levelled at the so-called "Cockney school" that included Leigh Hunt, Charles Lamb and the poet Barry Cornwall, but what were their shortcomings compared with the sensation-seeking of the Newgate novelists? "Did any one of them all ever perpetrate such an enormity as Mr. Ainsworth's Jack Sheppard," Barrett asked, "he, who for aught I know, may keep sheep in the wilderness."

Miss Mitford had actually read the book that was causing so much consternation and delivered a sombre rejoinder. Her remarks have been described as those of a fussy provincial old maid, expressing a sort of knee-jerk reaction to a book that appealed to the commonality. But Mitford was a more intelligent and worldly woman than that gives her credit for, and always, in matters to do with books, kept an alertly open mind. She felt, to her discomfort, that the subversive potential of *Jack Sheppard* was crossing a line:

> I have been struck by the great danger in these times of representing authorities so constantly and fearfully in the wrong, so tyrannous, so devilish as the author has been pleased to portray it in Jack Sheppard—or

he does not seem so much a man or even an incarnate fiend as a representation of power—government or law, call it what you may—the ruling power. Of course Mr. Ainsworth had no such design, but such is its effect; and as the millions who see it represented in the minor theatres will not distinguish between now and a hundred years back, all the Chartists in the land are less dangerous than this nightmare of a book.

4

The Play

"'JACK SHEPPARD'—HAVE YOU BEEN TO SEE 'JACK SHEP-pard'?" These were the words on everyone's lips in the winter of 1839, as "constant crowds and starers" gathered round posters for the play. John Forster noted the phenomenon with mounting annoyance:

> Jack Sheppard is the attraction at the *Adelphi*; Jack Sheppard is the bill of fare at the *Surrey*; Jack Sheppard is the choice example of morals and conduct held forth to the young citizens at the *City of London;* Jack Sheppard reigns over the *Victoria;* Jack Sheppard rejoices crowds in the *Pavilion;* Jack Sheppard is the favourite at the *Queen's;* and at *Sadler's Wells* there is no profit but of Jack Sheppard.

The play was particularly popular with young men of the working class, who treated the theatres as a sort of club and went as much to be seen by their peers as to watch the performance. Admission could be as cheap as a penny, so well within any servant's means, and among the crowds of youths thronging to see *Jack Sheppard* that season was Lord William's valet, François Benjamin Courvoisier, heading for the

Surrey or the Coburg on his Saturday evening off with a pal, perhaps, like James Leech, William Jones or Henry Carr, or scraping acquaintance in his unsophisticated English with young men like himself in the pit.

The various productions around the city competed keenly, each trying to provide something distinctive so that theatre-goers would go from one house to another, making commercially fruitful comparisons: Moncrieff's version at the Victoria not only had songs but an "ASTONISHING AND ELEC-TRICAL Representation of the GREAT HURRICANE on the River Thames"; another had a ghost scene, yet another a swordfight, and the pantomime version at Drury Lane had Jack and Wild turning into the well-known characters Harle-quin and Clown, with a final tableau held in front of a back-drop of Buckingham Palace, neatly referencing the Queen's forthcoming nuptials.

But the most famous adaptation, which had the best actors, catchiest songs and grandest spectacle, was that which opened at the Adelphi in October 1839, written by John Buckstone and starring Mary Anne Keeley as Jack and the popular comedian Paul Bedford as Blueskin. The script was lively and ingenious, paring down Ainsworth's complex plot to its essentials, and adding some unexpected humour. In the breakneck opening scene, the two orphaned babies were juggled about, and the fugitive aristocrat was chased across wooden rooftops to great dramatic effect; the storm on the Thames and Jack's escape from Newgate were other great theatrical set-pieces. Despite the fisticuffs, bludgeoning and, of course, throat-slittings that the story required, Buckstone managed to produce a feel-good entertainment, with some-thing for everyone: action, special effects, gothic scenes (Jack in Bedlam), weepy scenes (Jack at his mother's grave), men in drag (Jack escaping in a dress) and plentiful comedy banter. "I thought [Jack] was in Newgate," says a servant, with the reply, "He's let out for a few hours, but he's going back again after supper."

One of the great assets of the production was its star, Mary Anne Keeley, who was neither very young nor very slight at this date, but whose acting was so convincing that no one seemed to care, and who, like her co-star Paul Bedford, had an excellent singing voice. She had prepared for the role assiduously, taking instruction in wood-planing, pugilism and pocket-picking, and going on a tour of Newgate—just as Dickens had done—to try on the shackles which had been used on the real Jack Sheppard back in the 1720s. Facsimiles of them were made for the heart-stopping final escape scene in the play, rendered the more realistic because the business of picking the locks and filing irons was done slowly, so as not to look like theatrical sham. Mrs. Keeley had abnormally flexible hands and did all the stunts herself, making a set-piece of squeezing out of her manacles right at the front of the stage, in full view of the audience: "when I slipped them off it was no stage slip, but a *bona-fide* operation," she recalled, with pride. The audience loved it, and always gave her an extra round of applause.

It was physically a very demanding role, and apart from the soreness in her hands every night, there was a lot of climbing, jumping and dropping to be done (once from a ladder, which, when it went wrong, laid her up for two months). One young fan who used to hang around the theatre was backstage when the actress staggered off, completely exhausted by the escape scene. He was delighted to have to catch his heroine in his arms.

It was hard not to be beguiled by the Adelphi production, especially when Jack appeared at the Cross Shovels inn, splendidly dressed, with a beautiful girl on each arm and ready for the big production number that closed the second act, or when he gave his defiant speech before the Newgate gallows. "The fate of the Thief-taker and the Thief appears to absorb the entire attention of the crowded audience, as much as if a saint was being burned at the stake," one reviewer noted. In fact, such was the power of the play to "ensnare" viewers that he left feeling slightly vexed that Jack hadn't been rescued at the end.

Even Forster, arch-critic of Ainsworth's novel, went back to see the Adelphi production a second time in January, accompanied by Dickens. The novelist had written to the manager of the theatre, his friend Frederick Yates, to see if they could slip in for free. Dickens had almost certainly seen the production already that winter, perhaps several times; Yates (who had played Fagin in the first production of *Oliver Twist* the previous year) had no fewer than three roles in *Jack Sheppard:* John Gay, "Sam" the thug and the villain Abraham Mendez. Forster's official verdict on Buckstone's dramatization had been lenient, compared with his ferocious criticism of Ainsworth's work, and one imagines that in company with Dickens it was hard for him not to admit enjoying the sheer spectacle of the Adelphi's production, where, as he had to concede, "the scenic effects are really most surprisingly good."

Performances of *Jack Sheppard* at the major theatres were often packed, but Ainsworth received nothing except a one-off payment from the manager of the Surrey, John Davidge, who sent him £20, probably from a sense of sheer guilt. Ainsworth's text was mercilessly mangled (as was his name—one East End programme credited "Mr. Hainsworth's popular tale"), but he took it all with his usual equable spirits, pleased to have his story proving so very popular. He was glad to endorse the Surrey's production, much to the management's delight; they published his letter in their advertising, along with a careful note on the morals of the play, stressing that "depravity, however covered by bravado, is sure to entail compunction and punishment." There was nothing immoral about *Jack Sheppard* at all, the manager insisted: in fact, since the action took place so long ago, it could be said to offer an opportunity to muse complacently on "the change effected within a century; and say whether the upholding of the past to censure is not calculated to expedite the further improvement of the future!" This sophistic formula was summed up in Davidge's hopeful prescription: "In fine, Jack Sheppard is 'To all an example—to none a pattern.'"

The crowds that thronged the theatres hardly had such nice distinctions in mind as they jostled for tickets and the best seats. People went over and over again; a young boy called Henry Neville, the future actor, recalled later how he stole out of bed twice to go see the Adelphi production in the winter of 1839, slipping down the water pipe to evade his mother's knowledge—a very Jack-like escapade. And Walter Goodman, later a theatrical biographer, dated the start of his obsession with theatre to watching Mrs. Keeley as Jack Sheppard, a production which he saw on thirteen consecutive nights from the cheapest place at the back of the pit: "I became so familiar with the fascinating drama that at last I could repeat, almost line for line, everyone's part in it." The barrister John Adolphus admired the stage-effects enormously and went more than once to the same production that winter, while his colleague at the Old Bailey, William Ballantine, returned to have a closer look at Mrs. Keeley's "charming little figure

upon the stool in Jack's workshop." It's interesting that both
he and Adolphus were later involved in the trial of Lord William Russell's murderer, since the murderer himself would
admit to being another such *Jack Sheppard* fan.

The fact that the better dramatizations were endorsed—
even loved—by the educated classes made them even more
dangerous in the eyes of the play's diehard opponents. The
Monthly Review lamented that audiences of "what are considered well educated and superior classes" were apparently
enjoying themselves: "Performers of high reputation figure in
the representations; the plaudits of the audience are loud and
frequent. The very scenery of revolting spectacles and deeds
call forth the most rapturous delight."

The minor theatres and gaffs were another matter, and
if the reviewer from *Chambers's* had toured those houses, he
would presumably have been horrified by the much shorter
and coarser versions of Ainsworth's story, watched by audiences who booed, cheered and heckled as of right, and who
didn't need any critics to tell them what to like or not. Richard Horne was impressed by the sheer vitality of these places,
showing drama "which catches the manners as they rise, and
embodies the characteristics of the time" to crowds whose col-
lective responses awed him with their force. "Could all the
laughs be collected and re-uttered in a continuous volley," he
claimed, "the artillery of Waterloo would be a trifle to it."

A significant part of the success of *Jack Sheppard* at the Adelphi was due to the insertion of several show-stopping musical
numbers, with a bit of dancing thrown in for good measure.
The lyrics were taken, ingeniously (and one guesses at the
author's suggestion), from *Rookwood*, and included a drink-

ing song called "Jolly Nose," which was made into a rollicking solo for Blueskin in the flash ken. But the runaway hit was "Nix My Dolly, Pals, Fake Away," a catchy and charming tune, composed by G. Herbert Rodwell as a vocal duet between Jack and Blueskin, with a mixed chorus.[*]

Could anything sound sillier to audiences today than the words of this song (roundly parodied by John Poole and others)? But translated from cant, the meaning that emerges is far from silly or trivial:

> In a box of the stone jug [Newgate prison cell] I was
> born,
> Of a hempen widow [widow of a hanged man] the kid
> forlorn,
> *Fake away! [Carry on thieving!]*
> And my noble father, as I've heard say,
> Was a famous merchant of capers gay [dancing-
> master, i.e. hanging on the scaffold],
> *Nix my dolly, pals, fake away, [Never mind, pals, carry*
> *on thieving]*
> *Nix my dolly, pals, fake away.*
>
> My knucks in quod [fellow prisoners] did my
> schoolmen play,
> And put me up to the time o'day [taught me thieving],
> *Fake away!*

---

[*] The sheet music to the song is readily available online and the tune can be heard in antique musical boxes. One such instrument, dating from the mid-nineteenth century, can be seen (and heard) in a collector's video at https://www.youtube.com/watch?v=MOnLyRB1ovg.

No dummy hunter [pickpocket] had forks so fly
     [such nimble fingers],
No knuckler [pickpocket] so deftly could fake a'cly
     [pick a pocket],
Nix my dolly, pals, fake away.
Nix my dolly, pals, fake away.

But my nuttiest [favourite] lady one fine day,
To the beaks [magistrates] did her gentleman betray,
Fake away!
And so I was bowled out [arrested] at last,
And into the jug for a lag [prisoner] was cast,
Nix my dolly, pals, fake away,
Nix my dolly, pals, fake away.

But I slipped my darbies [shackles] one fine day,
And gave to the dubsman [warder] a holiday.
Fake away!
And here I am, pals, merry and free,
A regular rollicking romany,
Nix my dolly, pals, fake away,
Nix my dolly, pals, fake away.

"Nix My Dolly" was the big hit of 1840 and went on to become one of the most familiar songs of the decade, "as popular in the drawing-rooms of St. James's as the cellars of St.
Giles's," according to one observer, "whistled by every dirty
guttersnipe, and chanted in drawing-rooms by fair lips, little
knowing the meaning of the words they sang." The popularity of the song speeded "flash" into colloquial English, where
some of it remains today—*jug, kid, pal, beak, lag*—along with
other words made popular by the Newgate novelists: *togs, kid-*

nappers, *crib* and *lingo* itself. *Jack Sheppard* was turning out to have a peculiar ability to breach all sorts of existing social and cultural barriers.

The song was favoured by young and old alike. When Richard Harris Barham wrote to his daughter, anticipating a serenade on the violin she was learning to play, he joked, "Corelli or Viotti, I presume, I must not as yet expect, but I must certainly put in a claim for Jolly Nose [and] Nix my Dolly." You didn't need to have seen the play; the sheet music, lavishly illustrated with Cruikshank's production pictures, sold and sold and became so popular with organ-grinders and park bands that the Scottish poet Theodore Martin felt "deafened in the streets" by the tune. "*Nix My Dolly* . . . travelled everywhere," he remembered, "and made the patter of thieves and burglars 'familiar in our mouths as household words.'" To his understandable amazement, Martin even heard the song arranged as a chime for the bells of the cathedral in Edinburgh: "A fact. That such a subject for cathedral chimes, and in Scotland, too, could ever have been chosen will scarcely be believed. But my astonished ears often heard it."

Just how ubiquitous it had become within a few months is shown in a vignette of Dickens on holiday in Broadstairs that summer, recollected by a young friend, Emma Picken, who was the guest of their mutual friends the Smithsons. The two families spent long days together, playing games, swimming in the sea from bathing machines, sketching, picnicking and going on excursions. The novelist was skittish and flirtatious, and on one occasion he snatched Emma up and threatened to carry her right into the sea with him.

One morning, when they were preparing to go on an excursion to Pegwell Bay, Dickens came in flourishing a sheaf of ballads which he had just bought for a penny from a beggar in the street. Among the songs was a new one about the Queen's pregnancy, which Miss Picken priggishly decided might be too risqué for her unmarried ears. (There were plenty of raucous ballads around, concerning the Queen's marriage and Prince Albert's "big German sausage," so she may have had reason for caution.) But Dickens launched immediately into the chorus, to the tune of "The King of the Cannibal Islands":

> Go where you will by night or day,
> Through Britain's Isle the ladies say,
> Oh! The Queen is in the family way,
> The blooming Queen of England!

When the women in the party began to protest, Dickens gave them warning that he was determined to sing the new ballad anyway on the trip ("and a good many of the others . . . I am not going to invest my hard-earned penny for nothing"), so any objectors could go in the second carriage. The party subsequently divided along prudery lines, with only Kate Dickens and Mrs. Smithson riding along with the men. Miss Picken said later she was glad to have avoided being exposed to sauciness, despite the sounds of merriment from the other coach, with wafts of the irrepressible maestro's fine baritone followed by gusts of laughter. But Dickens clearly thought the girls were being affected: "It is in the vulgar tongue," he conceded, "but you are all so familiar with 'Nix my Dolly,' and other songs of that kind, that I daresay you will not be shocked."

It was a barbed remark, from several points of view, for "Nix My Dolly" was not only much more vulgar than anything Dickens had bought from the ballad seller, but so opaque that it passed as more proper. Ainsworth's song was a byword, and a fraud. And it preyed on Dickens's mind.

The corrosive effect on readers' morals predicted when the Newgate novelists had their first successes was nothing to the sudden alarm felt as *Jack Sheppard* fever hit the capital in the winter of 1839–40. "Public morality and public decency have rarely been *more* endangered than by the trumpeted exploits of Jack Sheppard," Forster warned through the mouthpiece of the *Examiner*, though he conceded that this had less and less to do with Ainsworth's novel itself: "All the original insignificance of the thing is lost, in the pernicious influences that are set at work around it."

Fraser's was equally foreboding; "There is no doubt," the critic John Hamilton Reynolds wrote, "that the popular exhibition of Jack Sheppard, metamorphosed from a vulgar ruffian into a melodramatic hero, with all his melodramatic virtues and splendours about him, in Mr. Ainsworth's novel, and its manifold theatrical adaptations, will tend to fill many a juvenile aspirant for riot and notoriety with ideas highly conducive to the progress of so ennobling a profession as that of housebreaking." A persistent worry was that the play would act as an animated handbook of crime, for "In every one of these places the worst passages of [this book] are served up in the most attractive form to all the candidates for hulks or rope—and especially the youthful ones—that infest this vast city."

At the beginning of December, Thackeray complained of the amount of publicity which the stage versions of *Jack Sheppard* were generating, and of the frenzy of interest in the hero's exploits. He also noted an unwelcome new development: merchandising. "At the Cobourg people are waiting about the lobbies, selling *Shepherd-bags* [*sic*]," he told his mother, "a bag containing a few pick-locks that is, a screw driver, and iron lever; one or two young gentlemen have already confessed how much they were indebted to Jack Sheppard who gave them ideas of pocket-picking and thieving which they never would have had but for the play. Such facts must greatly delight an author who aims at popularity."

Thackeray's fears turned out to have more substance than he could possibly have anticipated. Almost as soon as the story was on the stage, the term "a Jack Sheppard" began to be used freely in the press to refer to any ingenious housebreaker or nimble-witted young criminal. A ruffian who had stolen from his own father was called "A Young Jack Sheppard"; three boys aged ten, eleven and twelve appearing before the Central Criminal Court, who had cut the glass of a toy-shop window to steal toy cannons from it, were called "Juvenile Jack Sheppards" (they got one- and two-month prison sentences); and two other ten-year-old "Jack Sheppards" were said to have displayed alarming "cunning and hardihood" when stealing from a snuff shop in Tower Hill. A sparky nine-year-old who had been apprehended breaking into a house showed remarkable gall at the police station, singing "flash songs" and performing bits of *Jack Sheppard* for the amusement of the other boys in custody. The magistrate found this reason enough to send his case to trial.

The power of the story to rouse such youths was astonishing; it really seemed to speak to a whole class and generation of young people (specifically boys) who had not previously found much in the culture that reflected their own lives and concerns. In the 1990s, the critic Keith Hollingsworth asked why this particular mix of melodrama, sentiment, sex and song evoked such a strong and widespread response. It wasn't, he thinks, because Jack Sheppard represented a plebeian hero for the Chartist age, defying authority in support of the oppressed, but almost the opposite, that Jack appealed to the crowd because he stood only for himself: "Jack was not felt to be an enemy of society; he was a boy who scaled prison walls to be free."

"Again Jack Sheppard!!!" the *Examiner* shouted in December when three boys were apprehended by a sergeant in the middle of the night, hiding in the coal cellar of a house they had tried to burgle after the eldest of them had treated the others to a performance of the play at Sadler's Wells. The magistrate explicitly blamed the theatre for corrupting them, and gave a sombre warning from the bench: "that kind of knowledge," he said, "is calculated to bring you to the gallows."

Not surprisingly, some miscreants were quick to make the association themselves: it did seem to satisfy a gathering consensus that the story was leading people astray. A youth called Murphy, caught stealing from the warehouse where he had worked blamelessly for two years, said he had planned the robbery "in consequence of having read the novel of 'Jack Sheppard.'" An eighteen-year-old who had robbed a house in Woolwich while the family was asleep was found never to have offended before, but in court his father, a respectable shoemaker, lamented the way in which his son had fallen in with bad company at the local penny gaff, where the principal attraction was "a new version of the adventures of Jack Sheppard, the housebreaker." What was meant by "a penny gaff"? the magistrate asked, and it was left to the shoemaker both to explain this recent addition to the city's palaces of amusement, and to draw the moral that such theatres "did serious mischief in the town." Even his son, the novice burglar, wanted to blame the play for an almost instantaneous capacity to corrupt, saying that he and his friend had indeed cooked up their housebreaking plan on leaving the gaff, just after seeing the performance.

And you didn't have to be poor to catch the infection. Three youths in the Preston House of Correction in Lancashire, who came from privileged backgrounds "far removed from want" and were under sentence of transportation for a string of robberies and acts of destruction, said they hadn't needed the money, but did it "for the name of the thing," in emulation of "Jack Sheppard." Their ringleader had read the book and seen the play twice. "It excited in my mind an inclination to imitate him," the youth told the inspectors. "I read how he got into places; and I had a wish to try if I could do the same . . . When the scene is hoisted, he is carving his name on a beam which goes across the shop. I wrote 'Jack Sheppard' on the shop-beam, just as it was in the play. It occurred to my mind that this trade was like my own—a carpenter. I often thought about it when I was at work." He and his friends liked to think they were "getting like Jack and his companions. I am quite convinced that if I had never seen the play, I should never have got into this trouble. The play did me far more harm than the book."

A caricature in the press called "The March of Knowledge" illustrated the phenomenon exactly, showing a group of five boys walking along a street, the walls of which are plastered with posters for the play. They are "just come from seeing 'Jack Sheppard'" and are having the following conversation:

"I say, wasn't it well acted?"

"I believe you. I do likes to see them sort o' robber-pieces. I wouldn't give a tizzy to see what is call'd a moral play—they ar' so precious dull. This Jack Sheppard is worth the whole on 'em."

"How I should like to be among the jolly cocks; plenty to eat, drink and spend—and evry one has his *moll* too."

"Ar—shouldn't I like to be among 'em, in real arnest. Wot jovial lives they seem to lead! And wot's the odds, so long as you ar happy? Only see as how such coves are handled down to pouterity, I think it's call'd, by means of books, and plays, and pictures!"

"Blow'd if I shouldn't just like to be another *Jack Sheppard*—it only wants a little pluck to begin with."

All five—"That's all!"

A little pluck . . . it was a cheerful challenge.

5

The Investigation

AFTER FRANÇOIS BENJAMIN COURVOISIER WAS SO SHOCK-
ingly arrested and charged with his master's murder on
Sunday 10 May, he was kept at Bow Street and then sent to
Tothill Fields prison to await the committal hearings. When
the trial date had been set, he would be sent to Newgate.

Meanwhile, closely guarded arrangements had been made
for Lord William Russell's funeral, which was to take place
at the village of Chenies, in Hertfordshire, where the Russell
family had an ancestral vault. There was so much interest
in the case that even the empty coffin became an object of
curiosity, and the undertakers in Holborn found their premises thronged in the days preceding the interment with people
wanting to have a look at it. When it was taken to Norfolk
Street before dawn on the day of the funeral itself, Tuesday
12 May, there were already 200 spectators waiting to see the
cortège get under way. A short while later the coffin, now
covered in a purple cloth with gilt nails, emerged from the
house, was placed in the glass-sided hearse and set off slowly
up Park Lane and north along the Edgware Road, Inspector
Tedman and Sergeant Smith of C Division following behind.

The procession reached Watford at 10 a.m. and stayed an
hour and a half, by which time the town had heard whose

funeral it was, and when they set off again the road was full
of people, respectfully quiet and sober, who "appeared much
to regret the premature and lamentable death of his deceased
Lordship." In Rickmansworth, too, word had got out and
crowds were lining the route; it was the same all the way to
Chenies, where the funeral procession drew up at the Goat
Inn at about 1:30 p.m. The whole village was in mourning.

The family (its male members) had assembled at the rectory and at 3:20 p.m. the cortège left for the Anglo-Norman
church of St. Michael, built by the widow of the first Earl of
Bedford, and housing sixty-one Russells in its vault, including
Lord William's wife, Lady Charlotte, and their son George.
Tedman and Smith were at the front of the procession, in deep
mourning (giving Lord William what amounted to a police
escort), followed by the undertaker, then Lord William's
town and country agents, Messrs. Wing and Bennett (in silk
hatbands and scarves), with two mutes on horseback. Behind
the mutes—traditional funeral attendants, and only symboli-
cally, not literally, incapable of speech—were two pages, carrying a lid of feathers, followed by six of the most presentable
tenantry of Chenies, also in deep mourning. Then came the
hearse, flanked by porters with black silk hatbands and silk-
covered staves, and the mourning coaches. In the first was
William Russell, chief mourner, Reverend Lord Wriothesley
Russell (his brother-in-law and cousin, who was going to help
take the service) and Lord John Russell. In the second carriage were three more nephews of the deceased, Lord Edward
Russell, Lord Charles Russell and Lord Cosmo Russell, and
the final carriage contained Lord Alexander Russell, the Marquess of Abercorn and Fitzstephen French Esq., MP. For a
Victorian funeral, this was a restrained affair; the family had
asked for it to be conducted as privately as possible, with-

out the conventional procession of family and acquaintances' carriages after the mourning coaches.

At the conclusion of the lesson, when the coffin was removed from the chapel, Lord John stayed behind in the family pew, overcome by grief—not, as it happened, on account of his unfortunate uncle, but because he couldn't bear the thought of going into the vault and seeing again his late wife's coffin, placed there in 1838, nor his father's, which had been buried there just a year later. It wasn't the only part of the funeral that didn't go quite according to plan. On the way down the steps, the officiating clergyman, Mr. Bowers, hit his head on a projecting stone, suffered a severe concussion and was only just able to conclude the service in the vault and see Lord William's coffin laid above Lady Charlotte's. At this point, the strain of the previous seven days came home to William Russell, who broke down completely. His cries reached up to the chapel, and he was not seen among the mourners when they emerged, having been taken out to the rectory by a back door to spare him the ordeal of having to pass before the inquisitive eyes of so many strangers yet again.

The frustration of the family at the progress of the investigation was evident when Francis Russell, the Duke of Bedford, wrote to his nephew Lord William ten days later complaining about how little information they were getting from either the police or government sources; they'd heard nothing, in fact, beyond what was in the papers, "[though] we have hardly been able . . . to think of anything else, day or night." Sir Robert Adair, who had been following the coverage of the case very closely, also wrote to Lord William of his fears that Courvoisier might be acquitted due to the circumstantial nature of the evidence. His own valet, who was also Swiss, remembered a conversation with Courvoisier during which the latter spoke of how easy it would be for anyone to break into the Norfolk Street house, since the doors and fastenings were all old and defective. Sir Robert was hoping this might be used in evidence at the trial, although he realized that a clever counsel could twist it round, and represent Courvoisier's words as proof of loyal concern, not mischievous intent—undoubtedly the reason why Sir Robert's servant was never called as a witness.

The family's dissatisfaction was reflected by sardonic commentary in the press about police conduct at Norfolk Street: "Considering the modes of proceeding, it appears a miracle that anything has been found out," the *Examiner* remarked at the end of the second week. Back at the house, dozens of officers were coming and going, all intent on finding more evidence and all, presumably, keenly aware of the reward money on offer and the glory to be won if they could conclusively prove anyone's guilt. The building had been "really pulled to pieces" by the police, as *The Times* observed, as the bizarre treasure hunt for Lord William's missing valuables had continued apace, with more small stashes coming to light: part of the dead man's watch, bent out of shape, was found wedged behind the plate rack, a signet ring was behind a pipe, and one lone sovereign under the floorboards. Inspector Beresford had examined Courvoisier's box on the day of the murder: it had also been gone through by Inspector Pearce and Constable Frederick Shaw on 8 May, and nothing unusual found. But when, on the 13th, the third day after he had been taken into custody at Bow Street, Courvoisier requested a change of linen and sent his uncle Louis to Norfolk Street to arrange to collect some, the prisoner's box (unlocked and unguarded all this time) was disturbed once more. Tedman had directions to comply with whatever the prisoner needed and seems to have let Courvoisier senior up "to the place where the linen was" on his own, though nothing was taken out of the house that evening, to his knowledge. The inspector was due to go to Bow Street the next day, and intended to take the clean things with him then, but in the morning, when he and a constable (Lovett) went to fetch a shirt out of the box and shook it, something dropped out: a pair of very slightly blood-stained white cotton gloves. How had those been overlooked before?

The next day, even more suspiciously, Constables George Collier and Paul Cronin were sent to inspect the box and found in it, very near the top, a pair of handkerchiefs embroidered with the initials "B.C." which looked as if they had small drops of blood on them; there was also a new shirt which had had its sleeves torn off. Tedman said he had no idea how any of these things had appeared, or not been noticed before, but, given the open access to Courvoisier's room for almost ten days, it was not really very surprising. Collier said later that he thought Constables Shaw and Cronin, or perhaps Shaw and another colleague called Staple, had been rooting around in the box, but "I was busy searching another part of the room, and did not pay much attention to it." Courvoisier was far removed in Bow Street when these pieces of incriminating evidence materialized so suddenly; nothing could have made him look more victimized.

The valet was becoming the most talked-of man in London, with betting running high on the outcome of his trial, mostly in favour of an acquittal. A large number of people were convinced of his innocence, and he was receiving a steady stream of autograph requests in gaol, a phenomenon which the *Examiner* called "The Courvoisier Infatuation." Thackeray lamented how he couldn't get away from talk of the murder, even at the club—especially at the club: all the papers and broadsides were full of it, with ballads and commentary and speculation appearing alongside garish drawings imagining the serving woman's horror at finding the corpse, the police investigations of the house and, of course, the bloody deed itself.

The infatuation got the better of Lord Charles Greville, who paid to go and have a look at the prisoner when he was moved to Tothill Fields in the middle of May. "He is rather ill-looking, a baddish countenance," Greville recorded in his diary, "but his manner was calm though dejected, and he was civil and respectful and not sulky." The turnkeys, for a further consideration, told Greville that the prisoner hadn't been sleeping much and was "very restless," saying also that he had surprising bodily strength for a small man. One wonders what Courvoisier thought of being displayed to wealthy tourists in this manner.

The valet's status as a foreigner swung both ways: in the eyes of some, it meant that he was more naturally inclined to violent criminality than an Englishman; others felt sorry for a stranger in a strange land. He garnered a good deal of approval by waiving his right to being tried by a jury half made up of his countrymen, opting for twelve Englishmen instead, which was widely interpreted as a sign of good taste and respect for the host culture. In fact, in his conduct all through the investigation and his arrest, Courvoisier maintained the demeanour of an excellent servant, deferential and self-abnegating. A subscription was started among foreign workers in London to help fund his defence, while Sir George Beaumont had advanced the very large sum of £50 towards the same cause, clearly influenced by the exemplary conduct of the accused man's uncle, his butler. Other eminently respectable people were coming out in the valet's support, and John Minet Fector went as far as to declare that he would have no hesitation in taking Courvoisier back into his employment—should he be acquitted. The plea was not guilty. As Greville noted, "The circumstances of the case are certainly most extraordinary, and though everyday produces some fresh cause for suspecting the Man Courvoisier both the fact and the motives are still enveloped in great mystery. People are always ready to jump to a conclusion."

Both the police and the newspapers had been scrambling to find out more about Courvoisier after his arrest and discovered that he had been born and brought up in a small Swiss village, Mont-la-Ville, about eighty kilometres north of Geneva, in the foothills of the Jura mountains. His father, Abraham Courvoisier, a smallholder, was still alive, as was his mother, and he had two younger sisters and a brother at home and another sister in service in Paris. François had had a rudimentary education at the village school, then went to work for his father on the farm, but with no prospects for bettering himself at home, he followed his uncle's example and came to find work in England. This was in 1836, around his twentieth birthday. He didn't speak any English at all at the time and relied on his uncle's protection, getting work first of all as a waiter in a French hotel in London and then a post as footman in the establishment of Lady Julia Lockwood on Park Street, where his uncle's friends, Henri and Jeanne Pethoud, were the butler and lady's maid. Courvoisier wasn't officially paid anything for his work there, which was thought to be a fair exchange as he was getting free training and English lessons on the job. By Lady Julia's direction, Henri was told to give the boy "a few pounds at different times" in lieu of wages.

He must have made adequate progress with the language, because his next job was a good one, in a large and wealthy establishment at Kearsney Abbey, near Dover, organized again through his enterprising uncle's contacts, but with no French-speaking friends on hand. His new employer was John Minet Fector, the lucky young heir to a notable Dover banking family. Fector's father had wielded enormous influence as High Sheriff of Kent during the early years of the century, making a fortune from banking and trade and playing host to all the highest-ranking visitors to the port, including the Prince Regent, Louis XVIII and Lord Nelson. John Fector senior had shared the management of his business empire with an inseparable friend, George Jarvis, whom one historian of Dover asserts was his lover for many years (though both men were married and had families), and whom he made trustee of his estate and guardian of his eldest son. "Dover's godfather" was laying up great plans for this boy, building him a brand-new Gothic Revival mansion on a beautiful site by the River Dour, just outside Dover. Kearsney Abbey had all the most up-to-the-minute antique stylings: stone mullions, crenellations, massive doors, a circular turret. Inside there was an orangery and a billiard room, and ample guest quarters, all overlooking a newly dug lake and set in a beautifully landscaped wilderness. Fector senior died before the house was completed, but his son (only nine at the time) took possession of the property enthusiastically on his majority, and it became, essentially, a playground for the rich young heir.

John Minet Fector duly entered Parliament in 1835, aged twenty-three, as a Conservative MP, but there's no evidence of him being a very active politician. He seems to have been too busy spending the money he had inherited, having a

party for his twenty-fifth birthday in March 1837 that lasted
a whole week (and for which the local church rang a special
peal of bells), then going on a tour to the Continent and, very
exotically, travelling on to Africa for eight months.

This was the household where François Benjamin Courvoisier went to work as a footman when he was about to turn
twenty-one in 1837, and where he stayed for almost three
years. It was where he made friends with Henry Carr, and
with James Leech, who was one of the coachmen. Parties,
money, young, rich visitors: there must have been generous
tips for Fector's servants, long stretches of doing nothing
when the master was away and plentiful pickings from the
household's excess. When Fector was in London, he often put
up at Cox's Hotel or the British Hotel in Jermyn Street, where
Courvoisier got to know some of the other staff well. There
was also a property in Scotland, and one journalist tracked
down a Dumfriesshire local who remembered Courvoisier
dancing impressively at a wedding there, and presenting
his partner with a ring carved out of bone, which "did great
credit to his ingenuity and neatness of hand." Courvoisier's
dexterity was noted elsewhere: Thomas Selway, the butler
of Lord William's neighbour Mr. Cutler, had seen him shave
with either hand, and he was said to be particularly good at
tricks of legerdemain.

It's not surprising to find that Courvoisier missed the
liveliness of the Fector household almost as soon as he left it.
Moving to London must have promised progress, but he soon
found out that the pace at which Lord William's life moved
was far from exciting. A letter has survived, addressed by
Courvoisier to one of the higher servants at Kearsney Abbey
(possibly Fector's right-hand man, Henry Stone) on 28 April

1840, that indicates he was deliberately keeping his contacts there open, however much he protested his satisfaction with the new job at Norfolk Street:

Dear Sir,

You will think it perhaps a long time since I wrote to you, but I did not like to write before I was sure of stopping in my place. I have been to Richmond and Campden-hill, at the Duchess of Bedford's, for a fortnight. I have nothing to complain of my master, and he appears very well satisfied with me. I have not seen John, nor Henry, nor James, for a long time. I hope you and all your family are well. Remember me to all the servants at Kearsney, particularly Catherine, and if you go to Dover remember me kindly to Elizabeth, and all Mr. Straid's servants, and Mr. Sampson's, and Miss Bouche's. I hope I have the pleasure of seeing you in the month of July. My uncle is now in town, and sends his compliments. I have nothing more to say at present; but sincerely hope this will find you all in good health as I am at present.

Your most sincere friend,
F. B. Courvoisier.

This was written just one week before the murder of Lord William, and seems more than a mere exercise in politeness. It also seems to have been written in surprisingly correct English, given the ingrained faultiness of Courvoisier's written French. A letter written by him to his sisters in Switzerland on 13 April 1840 is full of all sorts of errors, to the extent of being only semi-literate (even if some of the mistakes were introduced by the newspaper which transcribed it in July 1840, as is quite likely). It was written from Norfolk Street, just two weeks into the start of the new job, and just before he was about to go out of town with Lord William for Easter:

> Chére Claris,
>   Je suis presque obblige de te manqué de parole, car jai beaucoup a faire apresent. Je pance que ma soeur sait que jai change de place. Jai quitte M. Fector comme tu le pansoit, mais pas pour me rentouere en suisse, mais poar arlez avec un vieux de 74 an . . .

The gist of the letter is that he has been extremely busy recently, for as his sister knew, he was about to change jobs. What she didn't know was that instead of heading back to Switzerland, he was in a new post with an old man of seventy-four (Lord William was actually seventy-two): "I don't have a lot to do, only, we do have a lot of visitors this week and you know that when you have to be a valet to three gentlemen and act as chambermaid for two ladies, there is always quite a lot to do, but after this week I won't have any but my old fellow, it is true that he is like almost all old men."

To his other sister, Clémence, who must have been asking when he was going to find himself a wife, he says, "You believe that I was cross when I read your little words of advice, quite the opposite. I thank you for the advice, and I can tell you that if I get married in England, it will not be with Henriet, even if she is a good girl." He wants to make some money first. "I know fine well that money doesn't bring a man happiness, but neither is it any use to marry and see oneself in poverty, and not to bring happiness either." He then partly answers

Clémence's enquiry as to what has become of the girls he has mentioned before as possible sweethearts, Henriet and Betzi: Betzi has gone to be a housemaid for the same family where her aunt works.

The letters show a somewhat evasive character, perhaps, slightly sycophantic and not very charming or cheerful. A boy with poor literacy skills, who was unlikely to go far. But nothing in Courvoisier's past made him seem like a potential killer.

Meanwhile, a concerted effort was being made to track down the items still missing from Lord William's inventory. The initial reward of £400 for information about the murder stood, but now the family put up more money—£50—to try to get a lead through the stolen goods. On Saturday 6 June, the following advert appeared in the press:

£50 REWARD—To Pawnbrokers, Silversmiths & Others.—Missing, from the house of the late Lord William Russell, No. 14, Norfolk-street, Park-lane, supposed to have been disposed of between the 24th April and the 5th of May last, the following articles:—Four silver tablespoons, old fashioned, with slight narrow stems, two of them are a little thicker than the others; four silver dessert spoons, plain stems, with double thread down the handles, front and back; four silver dinnerforks, plain stems; two silver teaspoons, plain stems, with double thread down the handles, front and back. The whole marked with a crest—a goat walking. Whoever will give such information as will lead

to the discovery and production of the above articles,
or any portion of them, shall receive the above reward,
on application to Messrs Wing and Twining, solicitors,
No. 1, Gray's-inn-square, Holborn.

There must have been many exclamations of surprise
around the nation's breakfast tables when this notice appeared: £50 for information leading to the discovery of a
single teaspoon! This sum was what a middle-ranking servant could expect to earn in a year, if they were lucky (it was
what the previous valet, James Ellis, had earned at Lord
William's; Courvoisier had been promised £40 to £50). The
murder wasn't mentioned at all in the advertisement, though
the victim was, and few readers would have been in much
doubt that the reward was aimed at flushing out any possible
remaining clues in the case. Find the cutlery and you'd find
the murderer—or his or her accomplices, at least.

William Harrison Ainsworth had not been brooding about
Jack Sheppard and the terrible name it had got for itself
among certain headline writers. He had already published
another novel by the summer of 1840, *The Tower of London*, and was busy writing two more, *Guy Fawkes* and *Old
St. Paul's*. When the last instalment of *Catherine* appeared
that spring, with Thackeray's very personal attack on him,
Bulwer and Dickens, he took it in his stride, not caring too
much when sales of his maligned book were so healthy. It
agitated Dickens, though, who was beginning to resent being
classed with the "Jack Sheppard school," and who wrote to
Richard Horne professing shock and surprise at the asso-

ciation of *Oliver Twist* with it. "I am by some jolter-headed enemies most unjustly charged with having written a book after Mr. Ainsworth's fashion," he complained. "Unto these jolter-heads and their intensely concentrated humbug, I shall take an early opportunity of temperate replying. If this opportunity had presented itself and I had made this vindication, I could have no objection to set my hand to what I know to be true concerning the late lamented John Sheppard, but I feel a great repugnance to do so now, lest it should seem an ungenerous and unmanly way of disavowing any sympathy with that school, and a means of shielding myself." This seems disingenuous, for it was perfectly natural that commentators would lump together *Oliver Twist* and *Jack Sheppard:* they were advertised and published together by Bentley, they had the same illustrator, they dealt with much the same terrain and class (the Dodger could be at home in either book). And the authors were great friends and would-be collaborators, or had been. But "disavowing any sympathy with that school" is exactly what Dickens was starting to do.

Dickens was, meanwhile, working on the story he had put aside in 1838, *Barnaby Rudge*, and had devised an ingenious animal character for it, a raven modelled on (and named after) his own pet raven Grip, acquired that year. Grip had a remarkable ability to learn and repeat speech, but was also gaining a reputation for casual violence, especially towards ankles, as both the Dickens children and his young friend Emma Picken noted:

Dickens was at luncheon at his house. He was preoccupied in his manner, but thawed a little when he took us into the garden to introduce us to his Raven, which was strutting about on the lawn, and muttering a string of slang sentences in the tone of a street-arab. He greeted me with "Halloa, old girl!" made some alarming pecks at my ankles, and altogether was unpleasantly familiar.[*]

Edwin Landseer had looked after the raven for his friend when he was out of town, but was currently in no state to do such favours. The murder of Lord William Russell had greatly exacerbated the nervous condition he had been in all spring, and at the end of May he collapsed completely. Lady Holland told her son that Landseer had seen Lord William, with whom he was very intimate, "frequently just at the time" of the murder and now imagined a similar fate for himself: "he is full of terror & horror, expecting an assassin to destroy him any minute. It is really very shocking." Gossip about this alarming state of affairs reached as far as Elizabeth Barrett, languishing on her sofa in Torquay, who heard that the painter had actually gone mad from fright. But could it be true, as she asked Miss Mitford, that this was because Landseer had been requested to make a sketch of the corpse before it was removed from its bloody bed? Or (Miss Barrett was appalled but intrigued to wonder) that he and the Duchess of Bedford had been locked in the room with the dead man when they went to the house on 6 May, and it was that which had sent him mad?

---

[*] Soon after this, the raven attacked the butcher's pantaloons so violently that the affronted tradesman promised to throw poison over the garden wall rather than risk another onslaught. Since Grip died the next year, supposedly from the long-term poisoning effects of drinking lead paint, it makes one wonder if the butcher carried out his threat after all.

It was a nervous summer in the city, for between Cour-voisier's arrest and the opening of his trial, another very shocking event had taken place, an attempt on the life of the newly married monarch (who was in the early months of her first pregnancy, though this was not yet publicly known). The young Queen Victoria and her dashing Prince Albert, accompanied by only four outriders, were driving their phaeton along Constitution Hill on the afternoon of 10 June when an eighteen-year-old pot-boy from Birmingham called Edward Oxford stepped forward and fired two guns at them in succession, missing both times. He was quickly apprehended by a number of outraged bystanders, and made no attempt to struggle, escape or explain himself. "It was I, it was me that did it," he announced, with a grin.

The Queen and Prince, meanwhile, had driven off at speed, not to Buckingham Palace, but to the home of the Queen's mother, the Duchess of Kent, in Belgrave Square, where crowds gathered quickly as the alarming news spread. The Queen was unhurt (it was never proven that there had actually been any shot in either pistol) but the shock to the royal couple, and to their entourage, was considerable. When Victoria and Albert emerged from the Duchess's house to return home, it was with an escort, not of the police or military, but "a vast number of the nobility and gentry, in carriages and on horseback," a phalanx of aristocrats, rustled up extempore by the Duchess to protect her daughter from further attack.

After the assassination attempt, the palace was inundated with messages expressing horror at the act, and gratitude for the sparing of the Queen. "It was indeed a most awful and providential escape," Lord Melbourne wrote to her; "it is impossible not to shudder at the thought of it." The Privy Council would examine the youth who had been arrested and make a full report to the House as soon as possible.

The culprit turned out to have had an unhappy background: both his father and grandfather had been violent men, locked up as lunatics. The teenage Oxford had moved with his mother and sisters from Birmingham to London a few years before to live with his aunt, who ran a pub; latterly he had been living in lodgings in Clerkenwell. Oxford had recently lost a job at the Hog and Pound in Oxford Street because of his unaccountable fits of laughing, which put customers off their beer; John Tedman, the inspector in charge of 14 Norfolk Street, had noticed this habit quite independently, as the boy used to work in the Shepherd and Flock, opposite the Marylebone police house. Tedman had judged the potboy to be daft but harmless; who'd have thought that such an insignificant-seeming loner would go on to plan an assassination attempt on the monarch?

But on 4 May, two days before Lord William's death, Oxford had bought two pistols and had been seen several times practising with them in the shooting galleries of Leicester Square. Then, in the first week of June, he bought fifty copper percussion caps and some gunpowder, and on the evening of the 9th showed his loaded pistols to several witnesses.

In the afternoon of the following day, he waited by the railings of Green Park on Constitution Hill, where he knew that the Queen and Prince Albert were accustomed to ride, and took his aim. Among the chance onlookers was a well-known Irish barrister called Charles Phillips, who was struck by the degree of shock everyone showed, "how the stoutest man stood appalled, and every face betrayed the most painful agitation." Why would anyone want to do such a thing? He hoped the young assailant proved to be insane, as it was worse to contemplate such an act being planned purely out of malice, or the desire for celebrity.

But celebrity seems to have been exactly what Oxford had in mind. In his lodgings, the police found a sword and cutlass, all the remaining ammunition that he had bought the week before, and a childish manifesto (apparently composed by himself, and full of invented names) for an organization to be called "Young England."* He later asserted that he had not intended to harm the Queen and from his cell in Newgate wrote an unhinged letter to the Home Secretary, claiming to be a prisoner of war and asking on what grounds he was being detained. But to his solicitor he could talk of nothing else but "the excitement he had caused in the public mind." Had his picture been drawn for the papers? Had he been "cried out" in the street? He "frequently rubbed his hands," the lawyer reported, "and exclaimed with great self-satisfaction, 'Nothing else will be talked of but me for a long time. What a great character I shall be!'"

"It's a great pity they couldn't suffocate that boy, Master Oxford, and say no more about it," Dickens wrote to Forster tetchily on 12 June. "To have put him quietly between two feather-beds would have stopped his heroic speeches, and dulled the sound of his glory very much." Calling him "mad" obscured something worse, the novelist thought: Oxford wasn't mad so much as monstrously egotistic, "brimful of conceit and a desire to become, even at the cost of the gallows (the only cost within his reach), the talk of the town."

---

* Not, apparently, connected with the later political movement of the same name.

Dickens had satirized that type of ambition in *Oliver Twist*, when the Artful Dodger's eventual arrest for the theft of a mere handkerchief arouses the professional regret of his friend Charley Bates:

> "Oh, why didn't he rob some rich old gentleman of all his walables, and go out *as* a gentleman, and not like a common prig, without no honour nor glory! . . . How will he stand in the Newgate Calendar? P'raps not be there at all. Oh, my eye, my eye, wot a blow it is!"
>
> "Never mind, Charley," said Fagin soothingly; "it'll come out, it'll be sure to come out. They'll all know what a clever fellow he was; he'll show it himself, and not disgrace his old pals and teachers. Think how young he is too! What a distinction, Charley, to be lagged at his time of life!"
>
> "Well, it is a honour that is!" said Charley, a little consoled.
>
> "He shall have all he wants," continued the Jew. "He shall be kept in the Stone Jug, Charley, like a gentleman. Like a gentleman! With his beer every day, and money in his pocket to pitch and toss with, if he can't spend it."
>
> "No, shall he though?" cried Charley Bates.
>
> "Ay, that he shall," replied the Jew, "and we'll have a big-wig, Charley: one that's got the greatest gift of the gab: to carry on his defence; and he shall make a speech for himself too, if he likes; and we'll read it all in the papers—'Artful Dodger—shrieks of laughter—here the court was convulsed'—eh, Charley, eh?"

Unlike with Ainsworth's novel, though, no one seemed in danger of taking the Dodger too literally. Dickens was a thorough satirist, both much funnier than Ainsworth and much more serious. There was never any danger of him becoming "bad enough to suit all tastes."

Called to give witness to his character at Edward Oxford's trial later that month, a former schoolmaster said that he had seemed "of unsound mind" as a boy, but not simple. He was an avid reader, it turned out: his aunt, with whom he had lived for two years, said he read "very much—generally sea-voyages," and his sister said that although Edward seldom went out, he used to get quantities of books from the library and "had, among others, the *Black Pirate* and *Jack Sheppard*."

So in the late spring of 1840, the nation's two most notorious young offenders, François Courvoisier and Edward Oxford, found themselves together in Newgate waiting to be tried one after the other in the new session of the Central Criminal Court that started on 18 June. Courvoisier was keeping up an appearance of perfect composure, and whenever asked about Lord William's death maintained deep concern about the progress of the investigations, and repeated a "most earnest ... declaration of innocence." He was receiving visits from a Swiss Protestant clergyman, Mr. Baup, whose chapel in Seven Dials was known to him (although there's no evidence he attended it regularly), and his reading matter was now exclusively the French New Testament: no more crime stories for him. The turnkeys who were on duty night and day reported that he was in good health and now had "no appear-

ance of disturbed sleep." Surely a guilty man would behave
differently?

Sarah Mancer and Mary Hannell, on the other hand, were
experiencing a different sort of incarceration, still living in
Norfolk Street, under police surveillance. This might have
been even more stressful than being in Newgate, since they
had to face crowds of gawkers and journalists every time they
left the house. Inspector Tedman and Sergeant Pullen were
in charge of the premises, and the two women went nowhere
without them. It was an eerie interlude for both, with no
work to do but also no leisure and the constant proximity
of so many reminders of their late master and his violent
death.

Sarah Mancer was under a lot of scrutiny in the press, and
was widely suspected of being just as likely as Courvoisier to
have wielded the knife over Lord William's blameless throat.
A rumour went round that she had been dismissed for theft
from her previous post by a Dr. Thompson of Kingston, but
Sarah denied any knowledge of him and, sure enough, when
Inspector Beresford took her to Surrey by train to test whether
any of the accusations were true, the Thompsons had no idea
who she was.

This did nothing to stop more malicious stories about
her appearing as the date of the trial approached: Sarah
Mancer wasn't just a thief but was in the habit "of frequenting houses of bad repute," and, perhaps most wildly, was said
to have been under Lord William's "protection," i.e. his mistress. Rumour-mongers were clearly responding to a certain
roughness in her manners, a lack of the deferential and calm
demeanour which Courvoisier could always summon. She
had been positively foul-mouthed on the day of the murder,
reprimanding the valet for not taking control of the situation,

and had given him that sharp push when he suggested trying to get a scruffy passer-by to take a message to Mr. Russell.

She had also been caught out in an act of petty thievery when, in the first days after the murder, the police started going through everyone's possessions. This had forced the maid to produce from her box a teaspoon and salt spoon which clearly she had appropriated at some earlier date. The casual purloining of things like this (that were unlikely ever to be missed) must have gone on all the time in domestic service and been, to a great extent, accepted as part of the job. But in the current circumstances it did not make Sarah Mancer look good.

It seems that many people, including the newspapers and the police, could only express their doubts about Courvoisier's guilt by continuing to cast equal doubt on Sarah Mancer's innocence, as if the murderer had to be one or the other of them. One Liverpudlian policeman called Dowling was so convinced that Sarah was "if not A Principal— perhaps actually THE principal actor" in the murder that he travelled down to London to attend the committal hearings, then began writing letters to the papers (under the pseudonym "Blue Rock") which roundly criticized the Metropolitan force for their incompetence, while repeatedly suggesting the housemaid's guilt.

The fact that Mary Hannell, the cook, was not treated with similar levels of vigilante suspicion or press scrutiny is slightly puzzling. Unlike Sarah, Mary Hannell wasn't questioned in very great detail at the inquest or during the subsequent police investigation; her reasons for leaving Lord William's service and where she might be going to work next were not demanded, and matters to do with how she spent the day of the murder were taken at face value, one could

say even less than face value. It could have been of signifi-
cance, surely, to know more about the friend she attempted
to visit that evening, but there's no record of this information
interesting the police at all. The friend lived in Chapel Place
off Belgrave Square, Mary claimed, but when she got there
and rang the bell, no one answered, so she came back home
again. As Chapel Place is well over a mile away from Lord
William's house, that would have been quite a brisk night
walk in the very short interval—forty-five minutes—of her
absence from the house, and nine o'clock was a late hour to
have been setting out to socialize at such a distance. "Off Belgrave Square" is also where someone had been trying to sell
a monogrammed watch seal, according to one of the anonymous notes. The fact that no one pursued these matters, when
all the best detectives in the Metropolitan Police were on the
case and swarming around Norfolk Street in a competitive
frenzy, is strange. Was there something about Mary which
made them rule her out of their suspicions altogether, just
as there seems to have been something about Sarah Mancer
that alerted their prejudices? Did Mary seem incapable of the
guile necessary to carry out and cover up a murder, or did
the simple fact that she was from Woburn, and known to the
family so long, incline the authorities to think her innocent?

Such was not the case for Courvoisier, though, who remained the prime suspect, and right up to the day when the
trial began, the scramble went on to find some absolutely
watertight evidence against him. Constable Collier of E
Division, discoverer of the shirt front in Courvoisier's box,
became convinced that the rest of the shirt must have been
disposed of somewhere, possibly along with the weapon used
to kill Lord William. His superiors organized (at some trouble
and expense) the dragging of the Serpentine and the reservoir

near Grosvenor Gate, which was the nearest accessible water-works to Norfolk Street (about halfway up the eastern edge of Hyde Park), then went on to search a pond in Green Park and the stream running southward out of Hyde Park into the sewer at Knightsbridge—all without success. The only thing they found was a pair of bloody stockings under a bridge, "supposed to have belonged to one of the numerous miserable females who infest the Park at nights." No shirt, then, "completely saturated with blood" and concealing a murder weapon, though that is what was reported in the papers one day, and had to be corrected the next. Everyone longed for a breakthrough.

The case for the Crown in the forthcoming trial was to be conducted by John Adolphus, a distinguished, elderly counsel, friend of Richard Harris Barham (and through him, later, Dickens) who had made his name back in the 1820s, defending the Cato Street Conspirators (who had planned to assassinate the Cabinet and trigger a national rebellion). Courvoisier's defence counsel, funded by Sir George Beaumont, was to be another "big-wig," Charles Phillips, a showman barrister, known for his florid speeches and Hibernian ardour, which he had famously used in defence of the Irish patriot Daniel O'Connell. He was a poet, too (author of "The Lament of the Emerald Isle"), and prided himself on his ability to recite verse, often moving a court to tears, especially, it was said, "the fair portion of his auditory." Phillips and Adolphus knew and disliked each other well: Phillips had once challenged Adolphus to a duel and travelled with him to Calais for honour to be satisfied with a cursory exchange of shots. Phillips's volatile temperament often got him into tricky situations like that, just as his showy eloquence and theatrical manner were legendary in the Inns of Court.

Courvoisier's trial could not start until the opening of the new sessions—18 or 19 June at the earliest—and was expected to take at least two days. Adolphus prepared for the brief by visiting the house on Norfolk Street and seeing for himself the bed where the corpse had been found, the disordered rooms and all the places where stolen items had been hidden. "I have not the slightest doubt of the wretch's guilt," he wrote in his diary, "but many are of the opinion that the Jury will not convict on circumstantial evidence, and I am far from being sure that they are mistaken." This would be the rub; as the trial opened there was "grave suspicion," but little else.

So long as the silverware was missing, the possibility remained that a second person had been involved in Lord William's death, who might have been the murderer. While it now looked as though François Courvoisier was certainly guilty of theft, none of the evidence so far proved him a killer.

6

The Trial

ON THE MORNING OF 18 JUNE, THE STREETS AROUND THE Old Bailey were thronged with carriages and crowds of people hoping to gain admission to the court, but the under-sheriffs had anticipated as much and were preventing anyone from getting into the building without a ticket, even members of the press. To maximize the number of seats available (and to control the crowd) they closed up the main door of the Old Court and erected rows of baize-covered benches against it; extra seats were also squeezed in wherever physically possible. Knowing that a lot of aristocrats were due to attend, a box was put aside for their use, but chairs were also made available for them on the bench. Thus the trial may have seemed to be presided over not just by Chief Justice Tindall and Baron Nicholas Parke, but sundry representatives of the class most threatened by the crime: the Earls of Sheffield, Mansfield, Lucan, Clarendon and Louth, Lords Rivers, Gardiner and Lennox, Sir Stratford Canning, Sir Gilbert Heathcote, the Dutch Ambassador, the Portuguese Ambassador and a whole flight of noble ladies "dressed up to the eyes, and furnished with lorgnettes, fans and bouquets," as the Old Bailey sergeant William Ballantine recorded. There was even a royal, the Queen's favourite uncle, the Duke of Sussex, who had given the bride away at her wedding in February. His Royal Highness spent the whole first day in court, sitting in the Lord Mayor's seat and taking "a great interest" in the proceedings. No wonder the court officials were "excited and perspiring . . . rushing here and there": they'd never had to manage such a circus.

In his introductory remarks for the Crown, John Adolphus set out some of the salient points of the case, with the aid of a three-dimensional model of 14 Norfolk Street made by C. A. Rivers, the court artist, to demonstrate the relation of one room to another, and the position of the house's four entrances. The inaccessibility of the backyard of 14 Norfolk Street, the clean state of the rear walls and the fact that the front door had been unlocked from inside all pointed to there having been no break-in, he said: "the house was therefore shown to be left with nobody in it but the servants who ought to be there, and the prisoner with the man he had named" (the visiting Henry Carr). These were the only possible suspects.

Adolphus opened the case for the Crown by emphasizing that Courvoisier had come to Lord William with a good character from highly respectable people and had a previously unblemished record, and also that all the evidence against him was circumstantial. But the amount of that evidence, and the many small peculiarities in the valet's conduct around the discovery of the crime, as well as the secreting of so many stolen items in places to which he had almost sole access, would need to be considered fully. Adolphus addressed head-on the matter of the bloodstained items found by the police in the valet's box (guessing that the defence would make much of it), and said he was not going to rely on "anything found in the box on any occasion": "Something might have transpired with respect to linen found . . . but he attributed no weight to it."

What he wished the jury to consider rather was "how it was that a good man became a criminal, whether suddenly or by premeditation—how it was that an individual of sound mind and untarnished character fell into temptation and committed crime."

How indeed. In the dock, Courvoisier was listening with great attention, writing notes on what he heard and generally giving the impression that he expected a good outcome. He pronounced his plea of not guilty in an impressively firm voice.

Sarah Mancer knew she was to be called as the first witness and had demanded an interview with Phillips in the lobby of the Central Criminal Court just before the proceedings began, to emphasize the falsehood of the distressing rumours that had been circulating about her character and past. Phillips, being a gentleman, assured her that he considered all such gutter-press reports despicable. But what he didn't add was that, being a lawyer, he would naturally take full advantage of them in court, and when Sarah Mancer entered the witness box she found him a formidable inquisitor.

First the prosecution and then the defence counsel kept her on the stand for hours, going over exactly what she had seen and said on the day of Lord William's death, and how she had described events to the coroner, the magistrates, the solicitors and the police. Adolphus was lenient and polite, but when Phillips began his cross-examination, he picked holes in the inconsistencies between her various accounts, down to very small details, upon which he clearly wished to establish doubt in her credibility, and perhaps in her innocence.

"Now, attend to me, on the oath you have taken," he insisted, "have you never said, 'I saw my lord murdered in the bed?'"

"No, sir, I never did—I never said his Lordship was murdered, the first time—I did not see his Lordship when I went in with the prisoner—I never said I did, to my recollection— I really was that frightened, I do not know what I said at the moment."

Phillips reposed this question six times, a relentless onslaught, trying to trip the housemaid into admitting that she used the word "murdered," not "killed" or "dead" when first in the room with Courvoisier. Though clearly very traumatized by this treatment, Sarah Mancer maintained reasonable control of herself: "To the best of my recollection I have always given the same account of what I saw in the room on the first occasion, as I have given today," she said. "It is a thing which impresses itself on my mind—I was that frightened, I do not remember what I saw."

Phillips did his best to make Sarah Mancer look like a rough and possibly disreputable young woman, drawing attention to the angry way she had addressed the valet and pushed him on the morning of the murder, saying, "What the devil are you doing there?" ("Feminine exclamation!" Phillips remarked, sarcastically.) "I am not in the habit of speaking so," the housemaid replied, "but I did not know what I was about."

Phillips then went through her employment record, allowing the jury to wonder what she had done during the two months' gap in 1838 between leaving the employment of Mivart's Hotel and beginning work for Lord William, when she lived in lodgings with a tailor called Don in Golden Square. Why had she not looked for a situation at that date, Phillips asked, adding, "You preferred living on your means?" As it was generally believed that female servants out of place were particularly vulnerable to corruption, this was a very pointed question, but Sarah replied in as dignified a manner as she could that at Don's she had acted as an unpaid servant while the people there and the head waiter at Mivart's all kept an eye out for "a light place" for her. It was the latter who eventually put her in touch with Lord William on his return from the Continent.

Mary Hannell wasn't treated with any such rigour. Her previous employment wasn't mentioned, nor the reasons why she was about to leave Lord William's service, or to what situation, if any, she was going. And of her movements on the night of the murder, the trial record is surprisingly thin: "I went out alone and returned alone" is all she told the court. No one asked her to specify where, or enquired about the "friend" she had mentioned at the inquest. Charles Phillips was the last person to let such things slip, which increases the likelihood that Mary appeared to the court beyond suspicion, that she seemed incapable of devising or carrying out such a carefully executed crime as Lord William's murder.

But the negligence over questioning Mary Hannell leaves many small matters unresolved. Courvoisier had locked, bolted and chained the front door behind her on her return, Mary said, but what was the cook doing coming to the front door in the first place? Was the gate to the area steps, by which servants would normally enter and exit the house, locked? When the valet offered to get her some beer later, he went out and returned by the area gate—the key of which hung in the kitchen—and said that he couldn't remember whether he had relocked it when he came back.

There are other slightly odd things in Mary Hannell's testimony, such as her description of the morning of 6 May, when she said she was startled by the housemaid's scream and rushed down to find her in the dining room (three floors down from the servants' quarters and two floors below where the corpse lay), where Sarah told her Lord William had been killed. This is quite different from Sarah's version, where she said she met Mary on the stairs to the attic. Perhaps trauma had confused the cook's memory; perhaps she had had a little too much of that beer and wine the night before; she certainly couldn't remember who sent for whom or how much time elapsed between one scene and another that morning: "I was very much alarmed and agitated—I hardly knew what I did." Courvoisier's behaviour—sitting down and writing a note, and lamenting the possible damage being done to his own future career—did strike her as a bit strange, but only when counsel suggested so. Sarah Mancer, a far more curious, observant and perhaps partial and volatile witness, volunteered her thoughts about the valet much more readily.

Mary Hannell confirmed that she had had no reason to fall out with Courvoisier in the few short weeks they had been employed together, and though she heard him make that remark about Lord William's supposed wealth, "I wish I had old Billy's money, I would not be long in this country," she had dismissed it as a joke. In her statements to the police, she always referred to Courvoisier simply as "the Man," instead of bothering to give him a name; one gets the feeling that she and he had very little interest in each other and intended to muddle along, as so many servants had to, by retaining a cordon of privacy and deliberate incuriosity around themselves. Her testimony in court emphasized this sense of leading parallel, but quite separate, lives; from her narrow bed in the attic, placed against the thin partition wall, Mary could hear every sound the valet made, moving about his own tiny room: "If he moved a chair or anything—if he had been walking about in his shoes, and I was awake, I should have heard

14 Norfolk Street, Mayfair, drawn by C. A. Rivers, the court artist.
Lord William's bedroom was on the second floor, facing the street.

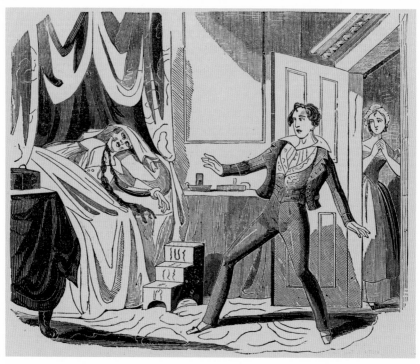

Newspaper illustration of the valet discovering the crime.

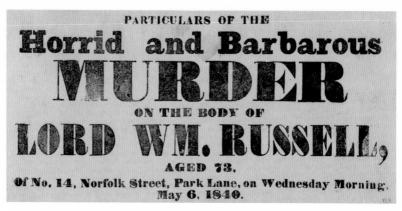

Broadside poster advertising details of the murder.

William Harrison Ainsworth in 1834,
the year of his first major success.

Charles Dickens in 1838.

William Makepeace Thackeray
in 1839.

Mary Anne Keeley as
Jack Sheppard in the
Adelphi Theatre's
famous 1839 production
of Buckstone's play.

Sheet music for
"Nix My Dolly, Pals,
Fake Away," with
George Cruikshank's
illustrations from
Jack Sheppard.

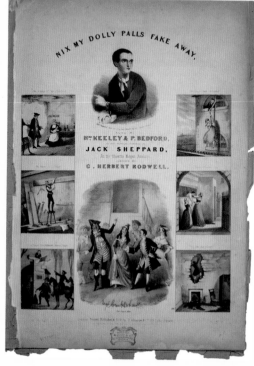

"The March of Knowledge"—a caricature of youthful fans of *Jack Sheppard*: "'Blow'd if I shouldn't just like to be another *Jack Sheppard*—it only wants a little pluck to begin with.' *All five*—'That's all!'"

Edward Oxford's assassination attempt on Queen Victoria in Green Park, 10 June 1840. The barrister Charles Phillips was an onlooker.

Dickens's talkative pet raven, Grip,
acquired while he was writing *Barnaby Rudge*.

François Courvoisier on the first day of his trial, sketched at the bar by C. A. Rivers. Madame Piolaine's evidence had not yet come to light.

A contemporary newspaper illustration of Courvoisier in Newgate awaiting his execution.

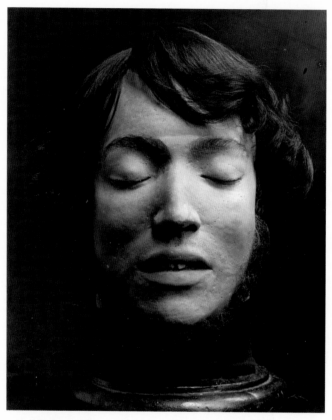

Madame Tussaud's gruesome model of the head of
Courvoisier, from his death mask.

him—I should hear him cough and blow his nose, if I was awake."

When the two doctors took the stand in turn, more small details emerged about the crime scene that had not been recorded at the inquest or at Bow Street. Henry Elsgood said that when he turned down the bedclothes and removed the cloth from Lord William's face, "the shirt-collar was wide open, and there was a sort of worsted network comforter over the chest, drawn up to the chin—I was obliged to divide that comforter before I could see the wound." This is a most peculiar detail to be making its first appearance at this late stage: there had been a comforter—a scarf—in the way of the wound. Elsgood goes on: "When I had done that I found the wound extended from the top of the left shoulder round to the part called the trachea—it went round to the right side of the trachea, dividing the throat—that wound was decidedly sufficient to destroy life, and immediately." A towel over the face, "tucked in within the sheets," a scarf around the cut neck: whoever killed Lord William didn't leave the scene in a hurry.

When asked how the unavoidable gush of blood from such a wound could have been prevented from making any marks in the room, Elsgood suggested again that the second pillow, which was stained with blood, "might have been held directly over the mouth of the vessel, directly the artery was divided." This was hardly convincing, but everyone in the courtroom seemed willing to accept it. John Nussey concurred with all of Elsgood's observations, and added one of his own, that he had been able to "see entirely into the wound almost from one extremity to the other." Neither of them mentioned the discarded truss that they had both seen near the body, nor the signs of "some slight struggle" Nussey had reported to the coroner. But one gets the distinct impression that, with such a packed court, and so many members of the aristocracy and the victim's family present (not to mention the Queen's uncle), issues of delicacy had kicked in which prevented too much being said about the corpse itself on this occasion. When, in the second day's evidence, Inspector Tedman began to describe the condition of the body when he saw it ("[the victim] looked as if he were asleep—his eyes were closed, and the tongue protruded a little way out"), the judge promptly shut him up, saying there was "no occasion for such a minute description of his Lordship's appearance. Nothing turned on it."

The last witness of the day was Constable John Baldwin, who, with his colleague William Rose, had been the first policemen on the scene on the day of the murder. But what began as a routine retelling of the events of 6 May ended, under cross-examination by Phillips, as something of a meltdown in the case for the prosecution: not only did Baldwin have to admit to making threatening remarks to the prisoner, and possibly trying to intimidate him into a confession, but Phillips was able to cast significant doubt on the accuracy of his observations and the order in which he had made them. At one point, having said he was downstairs "a few minutes," Baldwin had to admit that it had been more like fifteen or twenty. "I call that a few minutes," he protested lamely.

Then came the stinger. Asked by Phillips if he had heard of any reward being offered in the case, Baldwin denied it stoutly, and faced with the fact that posters about the reward were up in every station-house in the city in those weeks, he still claimed to have been too busy to have read them, or to have heard any professional gossip about the case. He had to amend this to having heard just a little gossip, but only with "one or two" colleagues; then this had to be adjusted further, under pressure from Phillips, to "I will not swear I have not spoken to twenty." Still he persisted that he hadn't heard anything about the gigantic £400 reward: he wasn't much of a scholar, he said rather desperately, and didn't read much. But news of it was read out in general orders, was it not? Here Baldwin's credibility collapsed completely, for he had to admit that yes, he had been present when the announcement was read out to all the members of the station-house— although he immediately tried to qualify this too by saying he hadn't been paying much attention: "It is a thing I do not take notice of, sums of money." The response to this in court rattled him considerably, and Baldwin went on the defensive: "I do not know what sum of money was named—I cannot tell how long it is since it was read out to me . . . I cannot tell if it was yesterday—I cannot tell you anything at all about it."

Well pleased with this, Phillips rested his case, and the court adjourned for the night.

Any optimism on the part of the defence was doomed to be short-lived, however, for someone had squeezed into the solicitors' bench during Baldwin's cross-examination, breathless and sudorific, who was privy to some startling and completely new evidence. Richard Cummings, a solicitor from Old Jewry in Cheapside, had received a visit that afternoon from two men he knew slightly, a Soho hotelier called Joseph Vincent and his friend Louis Gardie, both very agitated and insisting that he accompany them back to Leicester Square. A parcel had come to light, they told him, and no one dared open it without some law-savvy person present. When Cummings got to the Hotel de Dieppe, a slightly scruffy establishment in Leicester Place frequented almost entirely by expatriate Frenchmen, the proprietress, Charlotte Piolaine

(Vincent's cousin and wife of his business partner), produced a brown paper parcel that had been deposited with her about six weeks before and which had been locked in the cupboard she used as an informal left-luggage office. Prompted by an article in a French newspaper which Vincent had noticed, and which suggested that if the thief of Lord William Russell's goods was a foreigner, he or she might have used just such a place to hide them, Madame Piolaine put two and two together, and wondered if the package at the back of the cupboard had anything to do with the case.

So, in the hotel office, and watched by the proprietress and her two friends, Cummings broke the seal and cut the string: inside, wrapped in some clothes and padding, were a gold hearing aid in a leather box and a number of silver forks and spoons bearing a crest. The newspaper article was produced: these surely had to be the things the police were searching for, and for which £50 was promised? Madame Piolaine remembered clearly who had left the package: it was a young man who had been a waiter at the hotel about four years ago, and whom she had only ever known by the name of Jean. He had called in unexpectedly around the beginning of May and asked how she was. She didn't recognize him at first, but asked if he was now in work; he had said yes, "with a gentleman," not mentioning who. The next Sunday he had called again, and asked to leave the parcel. It wouldn't be for long, he had said: just till Tuesday.

Cummings, who must have been aware that Lord William Russell's murder trial was already under way and had some connection with missing silverware, decided that they should report the find immediately. After writing out a list of the contents—including a flannel jacket and a pair of dirty socks—and getting each of the four people present to sign it, he set off with the bundle under his arm, bound for Marlborough Street police court. He stopped briefly on the way at Ridgway's bookshop on Piccadilly to do a little detective work himself, and in the shop's copy of the Peerage found that the "goat statant argent" of the Russell family crest was indeed the same device as appeared on the spoons he was holding. Anxious now to be relieved of this potentially explosive package, he hurried on to the magistrate.

At Marlborough Street first an officer and then a clerk kept him waiting, but then there was a sudden urgency, and a message ordering him to go to the Old Bailey at once. Cummings jumped in a cab and arrived at the court at six o'clock. A note was sent to the prosecution, the awful package was taken off his hands at last and the solicitor slid into the court to hear the last minutes of Baldwin being "tossed and gored" by Phillips.

Phillips heard nothing about the new evidence that evening, but John Adolphus made the most of what seemed like a providential turn of events. Privately, Sarah Mancer and James Ellis were asked to look at the cutlery, and both confirmed it had belonged to Lord William; Ellis was able to identify the hearing aid too. But who was "Jean"? First thing the next morning, Charlotte Piolaine was taken to Newgate and shown a number of prisoners in the press-yard. She immediately picked out Courvoisier as the young man who had worked for her four years ago and who had left the parcel in May. She then retired to the chaplain's parlour, fainted rather dramatically and had to be put to bed for a while.

When Courvoisier spotted Madame Piolaine across the yard, he must have realized that the game was almost up. A couple of hours later, as everyone filed into court for the start of the second day, he summoned his solicitor and Phillips to

the dock and, bending down, whispered that he had decided
to confess to them, in strictest confidence, that he had indeed
done the murder. It was all Phillips could do to absorb the
shock of this without reeling, but more was to follow: Courvoisier said that, despite his actual guilt, and the damning
new evidence against him, he had no intention of changing
his plea. Phillips retired with his colleagues to consult (Sergeant Ballantine noticed him "much agitated" in the robing
room) and went as far as asking the advice of Nicholas Parke,
the judge who was sitting alongside Tindall, but not presid-
ing. The ethics of this move, and Phillips's decision to go
ahead with a full-throttle defence, were much criticized later,
but at the time Phillips said he believed his brief was to do his
utmost to get an acquittal for his client, and keep on arguing
Courvoisier's innocence as aggressively as before.

Judge Tindall was not inclined to hear any of the new evidence out of turn (although the court was beginning to buzz
with rumours by this time), and so the second day proceeded
as planned, with a whole host of police witnesses coming to
the stand, starting with Inspector Tedman. Phillips must have
been suppressing a certain impatience, hearing the inspector's
lengthy description of how and where the various coins and
rings had been found in Lord William's house and Nicholas
Pearce's minute analysis of which marks had been made on
which door, with what instrument, and by whom. None of
this seemed very relevant any more.

There was plenty for Phillips to develop, though, on the
theme of the inconsistencies in the police stories and the
suspicious nature of the sudden appearance of bloodstained
gloves, personalized handkerchiefs and a shirt front in Courvoisier's box, so soon after the announcement of one of the
biggest cash rewards anyone could remember. Tedman was

criticized for having let so many of his colleagues (and the three servants being detained at Norfolk Street) have access to the prisoner's room in the days immediately after the murder; it meant that almost anyone could have tampered with the evidence. Inspector Beresford was forced to admit that though he had satisfied himself there was nothing suspicious in Courvoisier's box on the first day, he hadn't unfolded every article; in fact "I do not think I took all the articles quite out." And George Collier, the constable who found the handkerchiefs and shirt front on 15 May, confirmed the impression that Lord William's house had been swarming with officers, all intent on finding "marks of any thing bloody." His candour about his discovery makes him seem like the victim of a set-up by one of his colleagues, for he only went back to the box "to see if I could find anything," but didn't have to search at all: the handkerchiefs and shirt front were very near the top of the box, and no one could have missed them, he thought, "if they had any eyes." "I should consider a torn shirt-front was a thing that would attract attention," he said, very reasonably. "It attracted my attention . . . if a person took each article one by one, out of the trunk, I do not think he could have missed seeing it, or the handkerchiefs either, if they had been there." *If.*

It transpired that almost all the policemen who had had contact with Courvoisier before his arrest had made threatening or aggressive remarks to him, which were thrown back at them by the defence counsel. It's interesting to consider that the source for this evidence can only have been Courvoisier himself, and also that Phillips saw no reason to withhold such material now, even though, by using it, he was impugning officers on behalf of a confessed (albeit in secret) murderer. Several officers bridled under the treatment they were receiv-

ing, being called "bloodhounds" and "ruffians" by the florid
defence counsel. When asked, pointedly, if he expected to
get any of the reward if the prisoner was convicted, Nicholas Pearce answered frankly, "Very likely I may—I do expect
it, in the course of my duty—if I should say no, I should say
false."

A series of witnesses took the stand in the afternoon, including Lord William's sister-in-law, Lady Sarah Bayly, and
his son John's widow, Lady Clifford, testifying to the fact that
the locket found in the pantry had been the one "lost" by Lord
William at Richmond, and that the £10 note in the valet's possession had been one given by Lady Clifford to Lord William
for a charitable purpose (to hand on to a former family nurse).
But the most dramatic moment came when James Ellis, who
had been called to act as the most trustworthy identifier of
his late Lordship's possessions, was shown several items of
cutlery, brought forward to the stand by Mr. Cummings, and
confirmed they were the missing pieces. This was the first
indication to the generality of what the rumoured new evidence might be.

Charlotte Piolaine, recovered from her dizzy spell, was
then called to the witness stand and made public for the first
time the events of the previous day, her suspicions about the
parcel in the left-luggage cupboard, the discovery of the silverware and her subsequent identification of Courvoisier at
Newgate. The accused kept his head down all through her
testimony; it must have been an exceptionally uncomfortable
time for him, with the whole court hanging on her words.

Cummings came forward with the pieces of cutlery again,
and now, with hard evidence that the valet had robbed his
master, Courvoisier's guilt began to look certain.

Phillips wasn't giving up, however, and set out to undermine Madame Piolaine's credibility as aggressively as he had done that of Sarah Mancer and the police. Leicester Square was notorious for illegal gambling dens, he pointed out—had the police raided her hotel recently? This "fishing" question made Madame Piolaine hesitate—no, she thought she could swear not.

"What did you mean by saying you *think* you could swear it?"

"Because I am never down in the billiard-room myself, but I never heard any noise [of a raid]." Encouraged to elaborate, she then said far too much: "I do not think there is any gambling-house in Leicester Place but ours—and ours is not a gambling-house."

Phillips went on to query the likelihood of anyone in central London not having heard "continual conversations" about the murder of Lord William Russell, the arrest of the valet and the massive reward for information. Had she not heard the murder cried round the streets, nor seen the numerous placards advertising the newspaper coverage? She replied that she didn't go out much, even on a Sunday, quickly adding, "I go to church sometimes." Did she not discuss the news with her husband? She didn't think so. They were very busy people, seldom dined together and went to bed at different times. He was, at that moment, abroad in France. He was often abroad, though he had been at home in May. Phillips pursued this tack; the home life of the Piolaines was getting to look promisingly strange. Was she never awake when her husband came to bed? Was she really too much occupied over the course of those intervening weeks to have a conversation with her spouse and bed-mate? "That is a question I cannot answer," the landlady replied. She must have wondered who was on trial now, Courvoisier or herself.

Adolphus (still ignorant of course of the valet's confession) requested the chance to close down these mischievous questions. There was no pretence whatever for calling the Hotel de Dieppe "a gaming house," he protested, nor for insinuating there was anything suspicious about the Piolaines' bedtime silences. "Do you, like other women, converse with your husband on things that pass, and think no more of it after it is over?" he asked, with no irony at all. Yes, she said. And, whether or not she had heard of the murder, could she—until she had seen him in Newgate—have had any idea that "Jean" and François Benjamin Courvoisier were one and the same? No.

Seven more witnesses came and went in rapid succession, including the print-seller whose brown paper had been recycled by "Jean," a washerwoman who had inconclusive information about Courvoisier's laundry marks, and the "aurist" who had made Lord William's hearing aid. Among these Soho artisans was Henry Carr, though why he was called at all and not questioned more closely about his long friendship with the prisoner and their movements and conversation on the day of the murder is puzzling. The unemployed man whom the police had originally considered a strong suspect said only this:

I am an acquaintance of the prisoner's—I was a fellow servant of his in the family of Mr. Fector—I think I have seen him wear a jacket similar to this (*looking at the one in the parcel*) in the service of Mr. Fector, but I cannot be positive—I called on the prisoner on Tuesday, the 5th of May—I left the house about a quarter or twenty minutes before six o'clock—he went out with me—I parted with him at the corner of Park-street,

a very short distance from the house—I saw nothing
more of him that night—I did not return to the house
that night.

And most strikingly, Carr was being called not as a character
witness (as the Pethouds and Lady Julia Lockwood were the
next day) but as a witness for the *prosecution*. One wonders
why, since his testimony is solely about the recently arrived
jacket that had been wrapping the stolen cutlery—and he
wasn't even able to identify that definitively.

There were two artists in court that day, making sketches
of the prisoner. One was the official court artist, C. A. Rivers; the other had come from Madame Tussaud's waxworks
exhibition in Portman Square, which for some years had been
producing a popular line in criminal effigies, arranged in
dramatic tableaux. In order to produce a model of the most
notorious contemporary criminals as soon as possible after
conviction, Madame Tussaud liked to capture some images
from life (what was left of it), and the courtroom was an ideal
place for unofficial sittings. The ardent sketching going on
could only have unnerved the prisoner in the dock. But not as
much as the sight of his friend Henry just a few yards away,
under the management of the prosecution. As the court broke
up on the second day, he scribbled a note to his solicitor saying, "Tell Mr. Phillips I consider my life is in his hands."

The jury passed the night at the London Coffee House, and
next morning had to push through the largest crowd yet of
spectators wanting to get into the Central Criminal Court to
watch the outcome of the trial. By 9:30 every seat was full
"and the most intense anxiety was manifested to witness the

appearance of the prisoner under the altered circumstances in which he stood." More aristocrats were present, including, for the first time, the Dowager Duchess of Bedford (who had last seen Courvoisier when she went to view her brother-in-law's corpse on 6 May), seven earls, eight lords, a baron, a general, several foreign ambassadors and ministers and a large group of MPs.

Weighed down by his private knowledge of his client's guilt, Phillips showed a certain overload of eloquence that day. In twenty years, he said, he had seldom had to address a jury under more painful circumstances, with the life of a prisoner dependent on so much conjecture and uncorroborated, last-minute evidence, all of which he considered far from conclusive. Given the rank of the deceased, the ghastly nature of the crime and the amount of sensational publicity which it had attracted, minds had been made up in advance against the prisoner, and the offer of the huge reward had ensured "his case had not been left to the ordinary instruments of justice." And, lamentably, class prejudice was the only reason why the government had been induced to offer such a reward in the first place, "as if the grave knew any aristocracy."

Phillips then harped on about Courvoisier's pious upbringing and love of his country, slightly misquoting Oliver Goldsmith's *The Traveller* to evoke the feelings of homesickness which had undoubtedly moved the valet to make his remark about Lord William's wealth. Phillips's rhetoric was particularly swollen at this point: "Ambition's vision, glory's bauble, wealth's reality, were all as nothing as compared to his native land. Not all the enchantments of creation, not all the splendour of scenery, not all that gratification of any kind could produce could make the Swiss forget his native land—

"Dear is that shed to which his soul conforms,
And dear that hill that lifts him to the storms;
And as a child, by jarring sounds oppressed,
Clings close and closer to its mother's breast,
So the loud torrent and the whirlwind's roar
But bind him to his native mountains more."

Indeed, Phillips contended, "There never dropped from human lips *a more innocent* or natural expression, 'I wish I had old Billy's money, I would soon be in my own country.'" The valet's bewildered behaviour after the murder also had a perfectly innocent explanation, he argued: was it not just like the loyal shock felt by onlookers at the recent attempt on the Queen's life, showing the traumatized reactions of a victim, not a perpetrator?

Phillips then went through the evidence, drawing significant attention to the fact that the prisoner's box had been searched at least three times without anything of a suspicious nature having been found, but then, on the 14th, the gloves were found, and on the 15th, at the very top of the box, lay two bloody handkerchiefs bearing the prisoner's initials. Courvoisier was then in prison and couldn't have interfered with the evidence himself. Why did the police keep going back to the box, which had been inspected on the very first day, and why had it not been sealed up and guarded? Some villainy surely had been at work.

And as for the evidence that had been rushed into court the previous day, who was this Madame Piolaine? No one had been given time to establish her bona fides or investigate her story, and Courvoisier should not be condemned on her say-so. Added to this, the maid was untrustworthy and the police had behaved like "miscreants." If they convicted the prisoner on the grounds offered, Phillips warned the jury, they would have blood on their hands themselves.

"The omniscient God alone knew who did the crime," he concluded, the murderer's confession of guilt still ringing in his ears. But the speech seemed to go down very well, if not with the jury then at least in the "most crowded court ever witnessed," who listened with breathless interest "and at the conclusion of it many of them present were affected even to tears."

When Phillips's speech was over, all that remained was for some character witnesses to be called for the defence: Charles Jennings of the British Hotel in Jermyn Street, and James Noble, Courvoisier's waiter friend there. Both vouched for Courvoisier's diffidence and modesty, "even simplicity of character," as Jennings said, reflecting the incredulity of many acquaintances that the valet was capable of such serious wrongdoing. Henri and Jeanne Pethoud then both testified to Courvoisier's good conduct, good temper and good standing with other servants when they had all worked in the same household back in 1836; more surprisingly, their employer, Lady Julia, agreed to take the stand and made the following statement: "The prisoner at the bar was in my service for nine months. I have had opportunities of observing him, and believe him to have deserved the character of a kind-hearted and inoffensive young man. He held the place of second servant in my family." The fact that such a well-known Mayfair lady—and *a personal friend* of the deceased—was prepared to support the prisoner to the last was very impressive—but this sort of endorsement was coming too late to help his case at all. The extraordinary amount of circumstantial detail was all pointing the other way.

The judge summed up and the jury retired for an hour

and a half, returning to a hushed court. "We find him *guilty*," the foreman declared, and after a short pause Judge Tindall asked if the prisoner wished to make any remark. Courvoisier said nothing, nor did he betray "the slightest visible emotion," *The Times* reported, unlike several onlookers. Tindall himself was becoming strangely emotional as he put on the black cap and addressed the prisoner in this way:

> François Benjamin Courvoisier, you have been found guilty by the unanimous verdict of an intelligent, a patient and an impartial jury, of the crime of wilful murder. That crime has been established against you, not indeed by the testimony of eye-witnesses, but by the no less unerring certainty of circumstances all pointing to your guilt, and sufficient to remove any doubt from the minds of the jury and those who heard this trial. It is ordained by God that the murderer shall not go unpunished, and that divine ordination has been fully exemplified and made manifest in the course of the trial, for, although your crime was committed in the dark and lonely time of night, when no eye but that of a watchful Providence could see the deed, it has nevertheless been brought to light in a manner clear and convincing to all . . . You selected the dark hour of night to deprive an innocent and unoffending nobleman, aged and infirm, of his property and life, and thereby destroyed, for a period, the domestic and social comfort of the members of his noble family.

"It is impossible for you to give any explanation," he continued, "your offence is so apparent, that an example must be made, for it has created a sensation and alarm almost unpar-

alleled among those who necessarily use servants." It only
remained for the sentence to be passed, "that you, François
Benjamin Courvoisier, be taken from this gaol to a place of
execution, and that you there be hanged by the neck until you
be dead, and that your body be afterwards buried within the
precincts of the prison, and may God Almighty have compas-
sion on your sinful soul." By this time, the judge's voice was
completely choked, but Courvoisier remained unmoved, and
was led quietly back to the cells.

As soon as the court broke up, rumours began to circulate
about Courvoisier's confession to Phillips, and newspaper
reports of the trial's last day included news of it alongside
the final speeches, verdict and sentence. Charles Dickens,
who was in Broadstairs that week and had been following
accounts of the proceedings closely, inferred from what he
read that the defence counsel had known all along about
his client's guilt, and became incensed by what he saw as
the lawyer's "wicked" and "wholly inexcusable" conduct.
On Sunday 21 June he wrote a note to John Black, editor
of the *Morning Chronicle*, accompanying a letter which he
"*very much*" wanted to have published in the paper as soon
as possible, and two days later a thundering denunciation of
Phillips by "Manlius" appeared in the correspondence column. "At the risk of giving some offence to the members of a
profession which is accounted . . . a highly honourable one,"
the anonymous writer complained, "I beg to propose to you,
and through you to the public mind, a few questions which
have been suggested to me in the reports of the late trial of
Courvoisier for the murder of Lord William Russell." Was it
justifiable, he asked, in the light of the prisoner's rumoured

confession to Phillips, for the counsel to cast guilt upon others and smear the police? Was it in any way permissible to use such exaggerated rhetoric as "miscreant blood-hounds" and the like against officers of the law? And how could Phillips be suffered to assault Madame Piolaine's respectability and integrity as he did, when her evidence had "so critically and providentially" appeared at the last moment, "thus seeking to render the discharge of that sacred duty to society which she had come there to perform, not matter of consolatory reflection to her, but a most painful and degrading circumstance?"

"Manlius" ended with a swelling tone of indignation, every bit as resonant as the advocate:

Whether Mr. Phillips was justified in appealing so frequently and solemnly to his God in behalf of a man whose hands he knew were reeking with venerable blood, most savagely, barbarously, and inhumanly shed—whether he was justified in doing this, and in plainly stating that the jury, in finding him guilty, endangered their eternal salvation, is a question in which I have no right or wish to interfere, but which I leave between that gentleman and his own conscience.

For myself, sir, I am a plain man, and perhaps unable to balance the advantages of continuing that license which is extended to counsel, against the disadvantage of restricting and confining it within more limited bounds. But the impression made upon me (and if it be made upon me, I have a right to assume it is made on many other practical men also), by the perusal of these proceedings, is—firstly, that I would never stretch out my hand to arrest a murderer, with these pains and penalties before me; and, secondly, that

no earthly consideration should induce me to permit
my wife or daughter to give evidence at the Old Bailey,
if any effort of mine could shield her from such a trial.

Two days later, "A Templar" wrote in response to this,
saying it was a jury's duty to convict only on proof of guilt;
a moral conviction of guilt on their part, or on the part of
the defendant's counsel, was not enough. According to this
anonymous respondent, Phillips was not only justified in defending his client to the hilt, "but in my opinion he was absolutely bound to do so . . . Though a man be guilty, that is no
reason that he should be convicted contrary to law." There
was plenty of correctness in this, but "Manlius" was moved
to answer back, repeating his former questions, with a special emphasis on the abuse of witnesses: "I recognize the right
of any counsel to take a brief from any man, however great
his crime, and, keeping within due bounds, to do his best to
save him; but I deny his right to defeat the ends of truth and
justice by wantonly scattering aspersions upon innocent people, which may fasten a serious imputation upon them for
the remainder of their lives—as those so profusely showered
by Mr. Phillips would have done in this instance, in the not
impossible case of Courvoisier having been acquitted."

Dickens was right to point out what a near thing it had
been. Despite Phillips's best efforts to discredit witnesses, and
despite the questionable nature of Madame Piolaine's parcel,
the valet was now on his way to the Stone Jug's condemned
cell to eke out the last sixteen days of his life. But not everyone considered that sentence just.

7

In the Stone Jug

WHEN COURVOISIER ENTERED NEWGATE PRISON CHAPEL
on the morning after his conviction, there was a palpable fris-
son, of the most negative kind. The story of how his trial had
been interrupted by the arrival of new evidence had created a
sensation in the prison "impossible to describe," as one journalist wrote: "Every prisoner, however fearful his apprehen-
sions might be as to his own fate, seemed totally absorbed by
the conviction of Courvoisier, and the singular intervention
of Providence for its achievement." The chaplain, Mr. Carver,
needed no other theme for his sermon, beginning with a verse
from Romans 6: "What fruit had ye then in those things,
whereof ye are now ashamed, for the end of these things is
death?"

The condemned pew in which Courvoisier found himself had been described by Dickens in "A Visit to Newgate"
as "a huge black pen," containing thoughts and feelings "far
exceeding in anguish the felon's death itself." The very look of
the chapel, to the novelist's eye, with its mean and functional
scruffiness, made it clear that a condemned man was considered half-dead already: "the bare and scanty pulpit, with the
paltry painted pillars on either side—the women's gallery
with its great heavy curtain—the men's with its unpainted

benches and dingy front—the tottering little table at the altar, with the commandments on the wall above it, scarcely legible through lack of paint, and dust and damp—so unlike the velvet and gilding, the marble and wood, of a modern church—are strange and striking."

As he listened quietly to Mr. Carver's sermon, Courvoisier bore no signs of what had happened overnight, when he had made a clumsy attempt to kill himself by cramming a towel down his throat. The turnkeys had interrupted him and he was now being watched with extra vigilance. No one wanted this prisoner to dispatch himself early; apart from it looking negligent, a suicide would deprive the public of the sight of justice being done. And there were other reasons to keep him alive: notorious criminals made lucrative business for prison staff, who frequently befriended condemned men and acted as their agents of communication with the outside world, procuring "exclusives" for newspapers and broadsheets, while whoever held the post of Newgate Ordinary (chaplain) actually had rights over publication of condemned prisoners' confessions, a valuable perk in cases such as Courvoisier's.

Up to this point, Courvoisier had hardly spoken about the murder, and despite the extensive police investigation and coverage of the crime, what had actually happened at 14 Norfolk Street remained to a large extent obscure. He had said nothing at his trial, beyond answering to the plea; neither had he broken down at any time, displaying the telltale signs of a guilty conscience. His last recorded utterance had been at the committal hearing in May. Now that the trial was over and his fate sealed, people longed to know the truth at last. Was he innocent? Was he a serial killer? Despite the guilty verdict, something was missing from the picture, especially in the matter of motive. People simply couldn't match the convict with the crime.

With so little time left, the governor of Newgate, W. W. Cope, and under-sheriff Thomas Flower encouraged the valet to dictate to them a full and frank confession. Courvoisier seemed ready and willing to oblige (just as he had always appeared cooperative and obliging to the police), and after several hours of interview his signed account of the story was released to the Home Secretary and the press on Monday 22 June.

"As I told you on Friday I began two or three times not to like the place," Courvoisier began. "I didn't know what to do[,] I thought if I gave warning none of my friends would take notice of me again." Prompted by dissatisfaction, then, he decided to stage a robbery at the house so that he could be discharged (presumably for some sort of negligence in giving imaginary burglars an opportunity to break in, as he had no intention of being blamed for it himself), and in preparation took the parcel of cutlery to the Hotel Dieppe on Saturday 2 May, saying to Charlotte Piolaine that he would call back for it on Tuesday. In the meantime, he had second thoughts about his scheme and decided not to go ahead with it after all, although he went as far as climbing out of the pantry window on Monday night to fake the jimmying of the back door.

Lord William's irritation with him the following day triggered his renewed resentment, and they had a further altercation at bedtime (about the inconvenience of forgetting to send the carriage to the club). Courvoisier said he then went back to his pantry and "stood reading a book for some time" until the bell rang at about midnight, when he prepared Lord William's warming pan, only to be told off again for assuming he knew what was wanted instead of answering the bell to find out. "He told me, rather crossly, that I should take more care of what I was doing, and what he was telling me, and pay him more attention. I did not answer at all, as I was very cross," Courvoisier said. In this petulant state of mind, the valet went downstairs and turned the dining room upside down. Lord William had meanwhile come downstairs to the water closet (wearing slippers, so his approach had been quiet) and surprised Courvoisier; there was another angry exchange between them, and Lord William said he must leave the house in the morning. It was only then, said Courvoisier, that he formed the idea of killing him.

This was the explanation which many people had feared: a disgruntled employee turns on his master with sudden and casual violence. The valet's account of the events immediately preceding the murder has many touches of plausible detail: "He opened the dining-room door and saw me. I could not escape his sight. He was quite struck, and said, 'What are you doing here? You have no good intentions in doing this.'" The valet said nothing but left the room, and while Lord William was in the water closet ("about ten minutes") waited out of sight on the corner of the stairs to the kitchen to see what his master would do next. Lord William went back into the dining room for a minute or two before returning to his bedroom, while Courvoisier watched him from the shadows. "I thought it was all up with me," he told Flower and Cope; "my character was gone, and I thought it was the only way I could cover my faults by murdering him," which he says he did about an hour later.

Courvoisier's description of the murder itself is emotionless and clinical, but also much less detailed than the rest of his narration: "I opened the bedroom door and heard him snoring in his sleep. There was a rushlight in the room at the time. I went near the bed, by the window side, and then I murdered him. He just moved his arm a little and never spoke a word."

It's characteristic of all Courvoisier's confessions that he is much more interested in explaining how he stole and hid Lord William's bric-a-brac than in saying anything substantial or particularly credible about his impulse to slaughter the owner. Readers of this first account were asked to accept that Courvoisier had very little motive beyond feeling "very cross," and attend instead to his hide-and-seek game with the police in the days following the crime. Courvoisier recalled with some pride that Lord William's watch and seal were hidden in his own jacket pocket until the second or third day, when the sweeps were in the house, and the fuller search began. This is when he tried to dismantle the watch in his pocket to make it easier to conceal, crush the glass and hide bits of it in his mouth, then burn the ribbon and hide the rest under the lead of the sink and behind the plate rack. "I did not know what to do with it, as the police were watching me," he said. The seal was still in his pocket; Courvoisier dropped it, covered it with his foot, then, in what he felt had been a pleasingly dexterous move, put it behind the water pipe while Inspector Beresford and Constable Cronin were preoccupied with the men taking up the drains. Similarly, he also managed to secrete some of the sovereigns and the locket under the floorboards and hearthstone.

The governor steered him back to the subject of the murder. Had he tampered with anyone's drink? Courvoisier said no, though he admitted to consuming plenty himself that night; the beer, the wine "and some more I took after the cook went to bed affected me." He had nothing to do with the gloves. He didn't even own any white gloves any more, he said, having given them all to the coachman James Leech when he left Mr. Fector's.

It's strange how much effort Courvoisier was putting into maintaining an aura of innocence, even after he had received the sentence of death. Having admitted to the murder, he was still unwilling to have any previous petty thefts laid at his door, and claimed only ever in his life to have stolen "one or two books" from Mr. Fector's library, a momentary slip, he implied, which could in itself be construed as part of a general push towards self-improvement, for who could object to an ill-educated young man craving books? In the same spirit of self-exculpation, he claimed that Lord William's locket, lost in Richmond, had fallen out of his master's coat while he was brushing it one morning at the Castle Hotel, and that he had picked it up and put it in his own trouser pocket "but had not the least idea of taking it. I intended to have returned it to his Lordship while I dressed him in the morning." Anyone listening to this story would of course think it strange that the valet didn't just put the fallen locket straight back in his master's coat, or that, having designated himself a safe pair of hands, he somehow couldn't find the thing the next morning, when they had moved on to the Duchess of Bedford's house at Campden Hill. But this was the sort of convoluted story Courvoisier spent his last days broadcasting from the condemned cell. His trousers were different, he claimed, but he hadn't realized that, and thought he must have lost the locket himself, so decided to say nothing about it (despite the fact that Lord William could talk of little else at the time). He would not have been believed, he claimed, which was true. After the murder, when the locket (by then wrapped in a piece of brown paper) fell out of his own stored clothes in front of one of the constables, Courvoisier again claimed that his innocence was so profound, he had no choice but to lie, "as if I told the truth I should not be believed." This yearning for his petty fabrications to be believed at this point, with the hours ticking down towards the drop, shows an interesting concern with his own image.

Mr. Cope and Mr. Flower took all this down, got Courvoisier to sign the statement and sent it on to the Home Office, where it became the "official confession" and has remained so to this day, despite several subsequent ones being made, and despite the glaring inconsistencies between all of them. For, once he started to tell his story, François Courvoisier showed a remarkable keenness to keep on telling it, to edit and augment it and respond to his audience's reactions, rather in the way that serial writers, like Ainsworth and Dickens, did well to keep alert to the reception of each monthly edition. Was he trying to elicit sympathy, hoping for some sort of reprieve or commutation of his sentence? That would not have been an entirely unreasonable hope. Influential supporters, such as Sir George Beaumont, remained unconvinced of his guilt, and he had several new supporters, such as Mr. Flower and Sheriff William Evans at Newgate and the Swiss clergyman Mr. Baup (who, as a man of the cloth, was allowed to visit him daily). To many of the public, he still looked more like a good servant than a psychopath, and even if he were mad, would that deserve the punishment of death? In 1840 there remained 200 capital offences on the statute book, but attitudes were changing, and in practice only treason and murder still attracted the death sentence. Even for treason or murder, the ultimate punishment was not always carried through. In January of that year, the very last sentence of hanging, drawing and quartering had been handed down to the Newport Chartist rebels—a shocking outcome, designed to remind other rioters of potential retribution—but even the Chartists had had their sentences commuted to transportation.

Details from Courvoisier's confession were widely circulated in the newspapers and found their way quickly into ballads being sung all around town, like this one, called "Verses on F. B. Courvoisier Now Lying under Sentence of Death for the Murder of His Master, Lord William Russell," which could be sung "to the tune of 'Waggon Train' ":

> A valet to Lord William Russell,
> He might have lived in honest fame,
> Respected by his fellow servants,
> And bear an honest name,
> Of Plate and Jewels he robbed his master,
> And in the house did them conceal,
> So cunningly did he contrive it,
> That quite secure he then did feel.
>
> It happened that Lord William Russell,
> Chanced for to go down the stairs,
> He caught him in the act of plunder,
> Which did his master sore enrage;
> Revenge and fear then filled his bosom,
> His wicked heart was bad indeed,
> His crimes to him they were laid open.
> Which made him plan the horrid deed.
>
> In the dead of night when in his slumbers,
> To his bedside he then did creep,
> With a knife the dreadful deed committed,
> Which caused many a heart to weep,
> But when that they had found him guilty,

The pangs of conscience he did feel;
Unable to bear the torment,
The horrid crime they did reveal . . .

A warning take then by these verses,
Think of the Valet's dreadful fate,
Let Honesty then guide your actions,
And in your stations be content . . .

There were other documents coming to light in the press, too; some, like the letter from Courvoisier to his sisters and the letter from him to the servant at Kearsney Abbey (both written in April), must have been acquired from the recipients. The same paper that published them (the *Southern Star and London and Brighton Patriot*) also claimed to have seen "some more letters addressed to the assassin, from his mother and sister—all of which give him useful advice," and "a letter from a sweetheart of his." The *Southern Star* had obviously got carried away by the opening words of this letter, "Chère amie [*sic*]," but it is clearly a message from a pious and affectionate aunt rather than a sweetheart, and expresses a strong wish for the worldly chapters of the young man's story to be over and done with soon. The content suggests that it was penned after the trial and sentencing, received by Courvoisier in Newgate and passed on fairly promptly to the media, for the paper (a provincial, Sunday one) published it the day before Courvoisier's execution. It must therefore, within a week or so, either have been purloined or copied on the sly by a turnkey, or handed over voluntarily by the prisoner, for the purposes of publicity. Is this another instance of Courvoisier trying to stage-manage his image from within the Stone Jug?

Mr. Cope and Mr. Flower had of course wanted to know

more from the prisoner about the mechanics of the murder, and specifically how he managed to effect it without leaving more widespread traces of blood. All that the official confession reports him saying on this subject is: "I took a towel which was on the back of a chair, and wiped my hand and the knife; after that I took his key, and opened the Russian leather box"; but the prison staff had clearly heard rumours of the "naked man" story (it had, after all, been hinted at in *The Times* as early as 8 May; it had also featured in several of the letters to the police during the investigation from members of the public trying to solve the crime for themselves) and off the record asked Courvoisier outright if it was true he had committed the crime naked.

Confusingly, two completely contradictory answers to this question exist. The more sensational one appears in *Recollections of John Adolphus* in 1871 (and elsewhere),* where the

---

* For instance, James Atlay's *Famous Trials* (1899) and Moreton Frewen's *Melton Mowbray, and Other Memories* (1924). Atlay says: "There is a well-known story that on the night of the murder a gentleman of high rank saw from a window in a house overlooking No. 13 [*sic*] Norfolk Street a man in a complete state of nudity washing himself in one of the bedrooms there. The house was not the gentleman's own, and to have given evidence would have compromised a lady, so he held his peace." Frewen's version has more elaborations. He says he overheard the story, when he was hiding behind an armchair as a child, that "a young lord from Sussex, Lord X" went to the Lord Chancellor during Courvoisier's trial and told him that "being with a lady in the house opposite, he had clearly seen a stark naked figure come for an instant between the curtain and the blind, which was not completely drawn down; this room he had since identified as the bedroom of the murdered man." Frewen's account is rather suspect, from several points of view. The person he heard relate this story was a Dr. Harrop of Brighton, who claimed that Courvoisier had been his own "favourite butler" "for many years," which is clearly not true. Small errors such as there being blinds in Lord William's bedroom

prisoner is reported as saying "he *had no clothes on,* he committed the crime in a complete state of nudity, and had only to wash himself at the sink on coming down." Less dramatically, in the week of the first confession, the *Morning Chronicle* reported Courvoisier telling the chaplain that he was dressed at the time of the murder, but "turned up my coat and shirt sleeve of my right hand." Here, he is not just clothed for the butchery, but keeps his coat on.

Neither of these answers is really credible, but perhaps that is because both could be partly true. Courvoisier might well have only turned up a shirt sleeve to take part in the murder, and a naked man might well have been seen covertly from across the road. Courvoisier might not have been the only murderer there.

On 23 June, Courvoisier's uncle visited him in Newgate and had a long interview, after which the prisoner called in Sheriff Evans and said he wished to make another confession. His conversation with his pious uncle had persuaded him that he must stop trying to disown his guilt and save his soul instead. Suddenly and surprisingly, Courvoisier retracted the whole "surprised burglary" story, and the scene of Lord William outraged in slippers on his way to the toilet. "Nothing at all of the kind had occurred," he said quite baldly. His signed new account of the murder was much shorter: his Lordship had been annoyed with him, but there was no real provocation or threat of dismissal, and it wasn't a spur of the moment decision at all, but premeditated by the valet for about a week.

(it had shutters and curtains) are more forgivable, since eighty-four years had passed since the crime.

He decided to stage the burglary, took a carving knife from the sideboard and went to Lord William's bedroom, where he found him asleep. The description of the killing is the only part that is particularly close to the first account, and just as uninformative: "I went to the side of the bed, and drew the knife across his throat. He appeared to die instantly."

This second confession was reported to the press along with a great deal of extra information garnered by Evans in a quasi-official interview with the prisoner. Since his conviction, there had been speculation that Courvoisier might have also been responsible for the unsolved murder in 1838 of a young woman called Eliza Grimwood, whose throat had been slashed in the Waterloo Road. Had he committed any other atrocities, previously undiscovered? No, he wasn't the Grimwood murderer, and no, he had not committed any other crime apart from stealing those two books from Mr. Fector. Yes, he was very sorry that Sarah Mancer and Mary Hannell had been put under suspicion—they were both entirely innocent of any involvement.

Evans pressed him further about the murder itself. How had the victim's finger been cut? Courvoisier's reply seems more speculative than factual, almost as if he wasn't there: "When he drew the knife across the throat, his Lordship's hand started up as if by a convulsion, and must at the moment have come into contact with the knife, and immediately fell back again, for death was instantaneous. His Lordship never waked." And the absence of bloodstains, how did he manage that? asked Evans. Courvoisier said simply that he wiped his hand on the towel, which he immediately put over Lord William's face. "He then, he said, went up to bed, but he did not sleep." No mention of washing. No mention of any struggle, any mess, or the "considerable effort," as John Nussey had described it, that would have been necessary to make that huge gash in the victim's throat, nearly through to the bone. Courvoisier made it sound almost elegantly done—"[I] drew the knife across the throat"—but such a wound could never have been inflicted casually; the knife must have been forced down hard, as onto a recalcitrant Sunday roast.

Evans was understandably perturbed by the surprising variance between Courvoisier's two accounts, especially about his motives, now that the valet said there had been no despair at the thought of losing his job, nor sudden rage at unfair treatment. The impetus, Courvoisier now claimed, came from quite another source. "He declared, and he wished the Sheriff to let it be known to the world, that the idea was first suggested to him by reading and seeing the performance of *Jack Sheppard*. The book containing the history of *Jack Sheppard* had been lent to him by one of the servants of the Duke of Bedford, and he lamented that he had ever seen it."

This was the true story at last, the valet insisted: he had been allured, and then corrupted, by the example of the enterprising thief. He had seen the play and he had also been lent the book by one of the Bedford servants, whose talk about how much better a deal they had than Lord William's household piqued his jealousy. Reading Ainsworth's tale of devil-may-care profligacy, Courvoisier took a fancy to the idea of living on his wits, and in a "first step on the downward path" stole his master's gold locket as a form of experiment. The ease with which he got away with this started him thinking about a more ambitious robbery in Norfolk Street and "to embark upon a career similar to that of the hero of whom he had read." He imagined that if he stole about £15 from Lord William to get himself started, he could travel from place to place, leaving unpaid bills behind and supporting himself on petty crime, like Jack Sheppard, then after about six months go home to Switzerland and no one would be any the wiser.

But if Courvoisier had been hoping to win sympathy for an appeal by offloading responsibility for his actions on to the year's most notorious youth-corrupter, he seriously underestimated the power of moral panic. When a version of this was published in *The Times* on 26 June, it created a sensation. So much had been written about the contagion of Ainsworth's novel, so many column inches had been expended on quantifying the evil impact of the theatrical and the broadside versions and the shows at the penny gaffs, that the public had got used to seeing Ainsworth's book blamed for a sudden and steep increase in petty criminality, but having responsibility for a *murder* placed at its door took criticism of the book into another stratum, as the *Examiner* was quick to underline: "[Courvoisier] ascribes his crimes to the perusal of that detestable book, *Jack Sheppard;* and certainly it is a publication calculated to familiarize the mind with cruelties, and to serve as the cut-throat's manual, or the midnight assassin's *vade mecum*, in which character we now expect to see it advertised."

The *Examiner* couldn't resist reprinting all the warnings it had issued the previous winter about the book and gloating over the criminal's newly revealed insights into the way it had inspired him: "The murderer frequently in the course of [his conversation with the sheriff] stated that Lord William Russell never walked down stairs, as seemed to be the general opinion, but was taken off exactly as he (Courvoisier) described . . . and he frequently, too, declared that he was indebted for the idea of committing the atrocious crime to *Jack Sheppard*." The paper even claimed to have found exact parallels between the crime and passages in the novel: "Curious it is that the very words used by Courvoisier, in describing the way in which he committed the murder, 'I drew the knife across his throat,' are to be found in the horrid book alluded to, in Blueskin's murder of Mrs. Wood . . . If ever there was a publication that deserved to be burnt by the hands of the common hangman, it is *Jack Sheppard.*"

The explicit linking of the crime and his book had a predictably devastating effect on the author, but Ainsworth would have been unlikely to respond in print if the *Examiner* hadn't made so much of the story in the week of its release. He had kept his distance from critics previously, but this onslaught was too public and too damaging to ignore. Affronted and offended, he sent the following letter to both *The Times* and the *Morning Chronicle*, claiming that the work mentioned by the murderer could not be his at all:

Sir,—A statement to the effect that the assassin Courvoisier in one of his reputed confessions, had asserted that the idea of murdering Lord William Russell was first suggested to him by the perusal of the romance of Jack Sheppard, and that "he wished he had never seen the work," having appeared in *The Times*, I have taken means to ascertain the correctness of the report, and I find it utterly without foundation. The wretched man declared he had neither read the work in question nor made any such statement. A collection of lives of noted malefactors (probably the *Newgate Calendar*) had, indeed, fallen in his way; but the account of Jack Sheppard contained in this series had not particularly attracted his attention. I am the more anxious to contradict this false and injurious statement, because a writer in the *Examiner* of Sunday last, without inquiring into the truth of the matter, has made it the groundwork of a most virulent and libellous attack upon my romance.

Your obedient servant,
W. Harrison Ainsworth.

But Sheriff Evans of Newgate responded robustly the next day, restating, not once but twice, the murderer's claims:

Sir—I observe in your journal of this morning a letter signed "W. Harrison Ainsworth," denying that Courvoisier had asserted that the idea of murdering his master was first suggested to him by a perusal of the romance of *Jack Sheppard*. I think it my duty to state distinctly, that Courvoisier did assert to me that "the idea of murdering his master was first suggested to him by a perusal of the book called *Jack Sheppard*, and that the said book was lent to him by a valet of the Duke of Bedford."

Your obedient servant,
William Evans,
Sheriff of London and Middlesex.

Ainsworth replied immediately to this, complaining bitterly at Evans's "impugning my statement respecting Courvoisier": "I beg to say, without desiring to question the veracity of any party, that my information was obtained at Newgate from competent authority, and is completely borne out by the murderer's last confession. Considering the number of confessions," he added sardonically, "it is possible that two contradictory statements may have been made, and with this remark I finally dismiss the subject. Your obedient servant, W. Harrison Ainsworth."

Unfortunately, the effect of his objection was rather weakened by the paper reprinting Evans's letter immediately below, leaving the reader to weigh the force of Ainsworth's Newgate informant (an anonymous "competent authority") against Evans's insistence that Courvoisier himself had repeatedly assured him that it was "perusal of the romance of *Jack Sheppard*" which had inspired him to commit his crime. Of course, both men could have been right if by "the romance of *Jack Sheppard*," Courvoisier had meant the history of the criminal contained in *The Newgate Calendar*—unlikely though it would be that the Duke of Bedford's valet actually owned a copy of that book to lend. Another possibility is that Courvoisier read a pirated chapbook or other, derivative, version. But none of these would have had any place in the market in 1839–40, without the lead, example and massive popularity of Ainsworth's book.

Far from "finally dismissing" the subject, the *Examiner* kept the controversy in the public eye for another week by reprinting all the correspondence and commenting on it with satisfaction. They welcomed Evans's authoritative evidence, though claimed to think it was superfluous:

> . . . if the statement of Mr. Ainsworth had remained uncontradicted, it would not have altered our opinion of the character and tendencies of *Jack Sheppard*. Had the book disgraced the time of Hogarth, the perusal of it would probably have made the first step in the great master's illustration of the Progress of Cruelty. As the passions are all excitable through the imagination, we

look upon this book as calculated to create a lust for
cruelty in minds having any predisposition to the vice.
Its tendencies are to familiarize the imagination with
deeds of blood, and to hold up to admiration the savage
criminals acting in them.

Ainsworth's defeat seemed so decisive that a note of me-
lioration crept in at the end of this extravagant diatribe—
almost certainly written by either Leigh Hunt or John Forster.
The "Jack Sheppard" effect had broken the bounds of anyone's control, and even Ainsworth could not be held totally
responsible:

> There is often in effects what was never entered into
> intention, and we acquit the author of having intended
> or foreseen the encouragement of cruelty, but the admi-
> ration of the criminal is the studied purpose of the book.

While the literary press tried to digest the news about *Jack
Sheppard*, François Courvoisier was adjusting his narrative yet again, and letting the Newgate officials pass on his
responses. The story wasn't getting through to the public quite
as he wished and there had been "false statements" published
in the newspapers that were bothering him. "If there are any
contradictions, it is because I did not rightly understand the
persons who questioned me," he said, suddenly playing the
"foreigner" card. The condemned man seemed concerned that
"the public think now I am a liar, and they will not believe
me when I say the truth," but that perception was hardly surprising when his story kept changing so much. In one of his
bulletins, he claimed to have hidden some of Lord William's
gold coins on his person between a second layer of stockings,

and still had possession of them when he was locked up at Bow Street. In Tothill Fields, where he was told (for the first time) to strip, he had placed his hand under his heel and concealed the sovereigns from view—ten of them—"in a paper under the thumb of my hand." He was able to keep them hidden, he said, until he was due to leave for Newgate, when he concealed them around the cell: one behind the bench, three on the lintel of the door, one on the window and five in the water closet. When this was published, it set off a rush of interest at Tothill Fields, but no one ever found any of the golden horde—or, at least, admitted to finding it.

Courvoisier's new emphasis on his skills of dexterity and craftiness—his Jack-the-lad credentials—seems more self-indulgent and self-aggrandizing than anything he had claimed before, more the utterances of a fantasist. Going back over the ways in which he outwitted the police, he said he had managed to move some things previously hidden under the stair carpet as he went up to bed, and also said he had been able to get to the pantry alone and hide the watch and ring there, though the police were all over the house, and two officers came in just afterwards to wash and shave at the sink. A notable feature of the different confessions is that they were for quite different audiences: Flower and Cope first, then Evans, and later the chaplains Carver and Baup—and he knew that everything he said would be widely reported in the press. The *Sunday Times*, known for its high circulation and sensational reporting, had run a huge spread of pictures, crudely generic but vivid, revisiting the crime, and showing Courvoisier in his cell. The only larger space given over that year to an image was that depicting Edward Oxford's assassination attempt on the Queen.

Courvoisier's evident pride in his palming skills now

raised suspicions that he had perhaps always been light-fingered. An unnamed source, claiming to be a friend of Lord William, told a journalist that Lord William had complained, just two days before the murder, that although his new valet had arrived with good references, "he feared he was a thief, as he had been continually missing property ever since he had been in the house." The confessions had also made John Minet Fector radically revise his view of his former employee, with Courvoisier's admission that he had stolen books from the library at Kearsney Abbey and "acted unjustly" towards the MP's mother, Mrs. Fector (though what he meant by this was never explained). Now Fector reviewed those years and recalled various times when things had gone missing. His offer to have Courvoisier back was beginning to look a bit foolish.

The publicity about *Jack Sheppard* animated some enthusiasts, who may have been hoping to effect a daring rescue of the prisoner. In the week after the trial, a young woman and two youths, claiming to be Courvoisier's sister and cousins, were stopped from getting into the gaol and having an interview with Courvoisier because the sheriffs suspected them of lying. In the novel, Jack's mistresses Poll and Bess smuggle him out of Newgate by deceiving the guards and dressing him in their clothes. Did the three unnamed young people plan an amazing Sheppard-style prison break for the valet? Or were they just thrill-seekers, trying to make contact with a celebrity? The sheriffs saw them off.

In the last days before the execution, the tone of Courvoisier's statements from the condemned cell changed significantly, becoming more personal (but still not revealing). He was seeing the prison chaplain, Mr. Carver, and Mr. Baup more than anyone else; he was praying, and reading the

Bible, and he had decided to come clean, *again*. Now he dismissed the quarrel he had with Lord William on Tuesday 5th as being insufficient motive for murder: "it was not worth the while to speak of it." It was purely "the evil disposition" of his heart that prompted him to plan the murder, prepare the fake burglary, get the knife and enter Lord William's bedroom: "I heard him asleep, and stopped for a while, thinking of what I was about to do." The voice of conscience spoke, but he hardened himself against it, "and threw myself on my victim." This is the first time he expresses any passion or exertion involved in the actual commission of the crime.

In the same edition of the newspaper appeared an account by Courvoisier of his early life, dictated to the chaplain and translated by the latter from the French (with, one suspects, some enhancements to point up the moral of his downfall). His parents were "very pious," Courvoisier said, and had high hopes for their favourite child, but "It has been my evil habit to have always a falsehood in my mouth ready to excuse what I did wrong or what I omitted to do; I fancied that it was more disgraceful to have a bad memory than to be a liar." "I was not immoral," he said of himself as a boy, "but I had no longer those holy inclinations in my heart." He was brought up as a good Christian, and "all who knew me believed that I acted uprightly," but since falling under the dominion of Satan he had broken every commandment, including "Thou shalt not kill," of course, but also "I have been in company with notorious debauchers." He deserved eternal suffering for his sins.

The astute Sir Robert Adair (Lord William's old family friend), though relieved that Courvoisier had eventually admitted to the murder, remained highly sceptical of the various scenarios that had been put forward, writing to young Lord William Russell, "he cannot have told the truth in his last and third confession." But the valet's last bulletin from Newgate, and a hand-wringing postscript published on the very eve of his execution, comforted some members of the public with its long-awaited signs of remorse:

> Oh! when I think how much evil I have done; I have dishonoured the name of the Swiss for ever. I have deceived those kind friends to whom my uncle's good character has introduced me. Yes; friends who, since the time of my arrival in England, have treated me as a member of their family. And my uncle—what have I not caused him to suffer! . . . I have deceived all my relations in my own country, who had so good an opinion of me . . . and to those young sisters who loved me as their own life, what a sad memorial I shall leave.

> SUNDAY 5TH JULY

Thackeray had been growing as tired as anyone of the prisoner's shifting story, but found this *cri de cœur* affecting. He must have read in the press of the murderer's claim to have been influenced by *Jack Sheppard*, but he had too much decency to crow over the distress this might have been causing Ainsworth. The murder put the Newgate-novel controversy out of the market for satire, and Courvoisier himself was now a genuine object of pity, as Thackeray wrote just a week or two later:

> Look at the documents which came from the prison of this unhappy Courvoisier during the few days which passed between his trial and execution. Were ever letters more painful to read—At first, his statements are

false, contradictory, lying. He has not repented then. His last declaration seems to be honest, as far as the relation of the crime goes. But read the rest of his statement, the account of his personal history, and the crimes which he committed in his young days—then "how the evil thought came to him to put his hand to the work"—it is evidently the writing of a mad, distracted man. The horrid gallows is perpetually before him; he is wild with dread and remorse. Clergymen are with him ceaselessly; religious tracts are forced into his hands; night and day they ply him with the heinousness of his crime, and exhortations to repentance. Read through that last paper of his; by Heaven, it is pitiful to read it.

Thackeray had decided to attend the murderer's execution, which was due to take place on Monday 6 July, and intended to join a group led by his friend Richard Monckton Milnes, whose plan was to spend the preceding night at his club and go on to Newgate at dawn. Milnes had voted in Parliament for reforms to the Punishment of Death Act all the way through the 1830s, but had yet to witness a public execution and was "anxious to see the effect on the public mind," it being such a relatively rare spectacle. Thackeray was also treating the forthcoming execution as an opportunity for research, thinking it could provide material for a series of "pleasant papers" he was trying to sell to *Blackwood's Magazine*, along with an essay on Charles Phillips's defence speech at Courvoisier's trial. "No politics, [and] as much fun and satire as I can muster" was how he imagined the articles, but the idea that he could keep a light tone on such a topic was perhaps unrealistic.

———

Courvoisier's multiple statements from Newgate hung in the air disturbingly, unprovable and uncorroborated. In Dublin, on tour with the Adelphi production of *Jack Sheppard*, Mrs. Keeley and her fellow actors experienced for themselves how the linking of the book and the crime was affecting the public mood. The company had had an excellent reception at first, and Mrs. Keeley was recognized everywhere she went for her depiction of the chirpy blackguard: "The town was full of it," she recalled. But after the reports in the papers of the murderer's confession reached them, there was an immediate effect on business. "We fulfilled every night of our engagement," Mrs. Keeley recalled, "but the houses were very poor." It made matters worse that the press was specifying that it was their own production, not just any penny-gaff rubbish, that Courvoisier had been influenced by, for, as the actress was sorry to hear, "[The murderer] says that the first idea of crime which he ever had came to him while he was witnessing the play of 'Jack Sheppard' at the Adelphi, and he had really been led into cutting Lord William Russell's throat through that play . . . When next I appeared in the character," she recalled, "there was quite a commotion in the house, ending in a complete uproar."

8

The Execution

FRANÇOIS BENJAMIN COURVOISIER, FOR ALL HIS AFFEC-
tations, was no criminal mastermind. He continued, however,
to be a celebrity. In the week before his execution, the public gallery of Newgate chapel was thronged with people who
came to watch him as he knelt at prayer in the condemned
man's pew. The sheriffs sold tickets for admission to the gallery, something they hadn't done for years, and on the Sunday
before the execution all the corridors of Newgate were full
of people trying to get in, with a high turnout of aristocrats,
including Lords Paget, Fitzclarence and Bruce.

It was here that Courvoisier, on the last full day of his life,
had to listen to Mr. Carver's further thoughts on his crime in
the traditional Newgate "condemned sermon," a sort of moral
summing-up: "You had almost reached the very verge of a
triumph that would have included the deepest sorrow to the
guiltless at almost the eleventh hour," the clergyman intoned,
pointing up the drama of Courvoisier's near-escape from justice. "So strong was the impression of your innocence, from
your long-established character for mildness and probity,
that a mortal stab was about to be inflicted upon the reputation of your fellow-domestics and other innocent persons.
You reposed in quiescent security of acquittal." But God sees

everything, and "in the wonderful workings of His providence, by a marvellous chain of circumstantial evidence, with
unerring certainty, fixed upon you the guilt of murdering one
whom every tie of religion and morality bound you to love,
reverence, and respect." Naturally enough, Mr. Carver made
no reference to the influence of other providential interven-
tions, such as the £50 reward.

The chaplain didn't scant his own part in the death-row
drama, his daily visits to the prisoner and the extraction of
something like an expression of remorse for the murder. But
it hadn't been an entirely satisfactory process, Carver had to
admit; Courvoisier had owned up to the crime, "but the evasions, subterfuges, and inconsistencies which have appeared
in your recorded verbal statements on minor details have
very naturally induced the fear that 'your heart is not right in
the sight of God.' "

The prisoner kept his eyes cast down throughout the
service, but behind him was seated his clownish shadow,
Edward Oxford, flanked by two turnkeys. Oxford's trial for
treason had been postponed until 9 July, but there seemed
every probability that he too would take his place in the condemned pew in due course. He seemed to pay attention to
what was being said and sometimes joined in the responses,
but when the chaplain was uttering the prayer for the safety
of the Queen, he looked up and sniggered.

Courvoisier's final hours didn't pass without more drama.
Last thing at night, when the governor went to Courvoisier's
cell and told him it was time to strip and go to bed, the prisoner hesitated and seemed put out by the idea of a search.
Suspecting that he had hidden something in his mattress with
which to kill himself, the turnkeys quickly changed the bed

and inspected the prisoner's clothes, and found secreted in his jacket pocket a thin strip of cloth. Where had he got it, and what was he proposing to do with it? Cope asked. Courvoisier said that he had stripped some material from the inside seam of his trousers (while in the water closet) and had been planning to make a ligature, then tie it tightly round his arm and open a vein in the night, to bleed himself to death. He said he had been looking for a way to kill himself all the time he had been in gaol and had hidden a sharpened stick from the fire in his mattress to use for the piercing.

Nothing was found in the mattress, however, prompting this weary remark in one of the newspapers which reported the incident: "in the removal it might have been lost; or the prisoner might have indulged himself with another lie before his exit."

A few evenings before this, Charles Dickens's friend Mrs. Charles Smithson had friends to dine, including her brother the novelist Thomas Thompson, and their young family friend Emma Picken, who thirty years later recorded what was said. After dinner, the party in the drawing room was disturbed by the arrival of Charles's older brother Fred Dickens, "looking even more discontented than usual," and under a cloud of preoccupation. When asked what was the matter, Fred responded with an elaborate charade, waving his hands up and down "like a mesmerist" before breaking into an extemporized chant:

I'm unaware of any care, but I'll make you stare
So now prepare, for news most rare,

I'm going to share, a window where
I can convaniently [*sic*] behold Courvoisi-er-er-er
Receive his well-earned hanging there.

Emma Picken recalled the subsequent conversation:

"What?" exclaimed Dickens in surprise. "You're never going to be such an idiot! Whence comes this morbid craving to gloat over such a loathsome exhibition."

"Thackeray is going, I believe, and I am joining a select circle of reporters. It's an excitement, it will be quite a new sensation, and will arouse my slumbering energies, which are as stagnant as ditch-water."

"You'll be squeamish for a week afterwards," remarked Mr. Thompson quietly.

"Have you ever seen a man hanged?" asked Fred.

"No, but I've seen a man guillotined."

"Ugh!" cried Dickens with a shudder of disgust. "That's such a messy business, all gore and sawdust. The inverted rope-dance is cleaner though less impressive. I'd keep away from such a hideous *spectácle* from principle. I'm not sure that we ought to dispose of even murderers in such barbarous ways."

Dickens had recently become interested in phrenology through his friend Dr. John Elliotson, who promoted it assiduously as a serious science (and who was also a leading demonstrator of mesmerism; Dickens and Ainsworth had gone together to see him mesmerize the Okey sisters in 1838). Elliotson asserted that you could deduce a subject's mental capacities and predispositions from the exact size and shape of the contours of the head, and was interested in examining the skulls of criminals such as Courvoisier. "If there's any truth in phrenology, if physiognomy is in the least an index of the inward tendencies," Dickens said to Fred, "there are unfortunate wretches born with murderous propensities. Self-defence and public safety demand that these unfortunate brutes should be exterminated, but I pity the poor brutes notwithstanding."

"Charles," said Fred, with his oily laugh, "you are capable of imitating the Scotch minister who prayed for the 'puir de'il [poor devil].'"

"Well, yes, I think the 'puir de'il' the unhappiest wretch under heaven. I am inclined to think with Festus that even he will repent and be forgiven in the end."

Fred got up to leave soon after, but his brother was now in a satirical mood. Thomas Thompson had for many years employed a Swiss valet called Jacques, and as Dickens left the room, he tiptoed over in an elaborate pantomime of terror and stage-whispered: "Friend, be advised,—look to't! See that thou lock, bolt, and bar thy chamber door from henceforth. I tremble for thee! Perchance the 'melancholy Jacques' is even now sharpening a *carver* for thy guileless throat. Remember! Be advised! I give thee good den!" He tousled his hair to make it stand on end and tiptoed out, with his finger to his lips, much to the amusement of Miss Picken and the Smithsons: "the portentous gloom with which he shook his dishevelled locks as he finally made his exit, were greeted with a burst of laughter."

Having raised so many objections to Fred attending Courvoisier's execution, it is something of a surprise to find that on the night of 5 July, Dickens suddenly decided to experi-

ence the "loathsome exhibition" first-hand himself. At the end
of a pleasant evening at home in Devonshire Terrace with
his wife, his sister Fanny, brother-in-law Henry Burnett and
friend Daniel Maclise, he suggested that they all go over to
Newgate to see "what is being done in the way of preparation." Fanny and Kate Dickens both objected strongly to the
scheme, but Maclise was enthusiastic, pointing out that it
was a fine night and a short walk, and Dickens needed no
other encouragement. Before he knew it, Burnett was being
whisked out of the house on what was to prove a long and
disquieting nocturnal adventure.

They got to Newgate by eleven o'clock, but barriers were
already in place and spectators camped out, two or three
deep, to secure the best viewing places. Fascinated by the
scene, Dickens led his party on a slow walk around the area,
as far as Smithfield, but all the time the flow of people going
the other way, towards Newgate, was increasing; Burnett
had to use his arms to make his way, as if he were swimming
against a tide. This was their first intimation of how many
Londoners were gathering to watch Courvoisier hang. Vast
crowds at Newgate executions were commonplace (in 1806,
twenty-eight people died in the crush there), but this seemed
completely out of the ordinary; later estimates, though they
varied widely,* agreed a consensus of around 40,000. The
mass of bodies was alarming to behold and almost impossible
to navigate through: "It might now be said that we were no
more in a stream but in a narrow river," Burnett recalled, "as
we neared the Gaol we managed to turn aside and save our-
selves from being overwhelmed."

By the time Dickens's party got back to Newgate Yard,

_____
* From 20,000 to 50,000.

it was one o'clock in the morning. Burnett was keen to go home; his wife had been expecting him by midnight, and he was finding the swelling crowd disgusting. But Dickens had woken up to the occasion and now wanted to stay out all night and witness the execution, his first. For "Boz" it was too rich material to forgo: "Just once I should like to watch a scene like this, and see the end of the Drama," he said as he went off to negotiate for the last available place left to rent, an upper room in a house facing the "drop." Some of the positions opposite the prison fetched as much as five guineas on occasions such as this, and in one of the houses, the owners had removed the windows to allow more gawking space.

Scuffles were already breaking out, and there were sounds of laughter in the dark from groups of people passing the long hours in the middle of the night drinking, playing cards and gambling. But Dickens was fully absorbed, and settled down to watch all the goings-on in the "pit" from his elevated box.

It was a long night. At around two in the morning, a team of horses was led into the yard to move pieces of the scaffold, and an ominous hammering began. The surrounding roads, from Giltspur Street to Ludgate Hill, were packed, and as dawn approached the crowd seemed to become more animated, "a rocking surging sea of degradation, degeneracy and baseness—a sink of human filth!" as Burnett exclaimed. There were pickpockets everywhere, making the most of a feast, and sensitive Burnett was particularly struck by how coarse and "beastly" a lot of the women were, and how many of them, faint from being squeezed in the throng, but with no room to fall down, remained "jambed like a wedge in human flesh," unconscious but upright. He saw several attempts at raising women up above the heads of the crowd for a better view (rather like at modern-day music festivals), but with so little space to manoeuvre, "slowly a hand here and there was seen released, until at length the bundle of rags disappeared."

As the workmen finished constructing the gallows, Burnett felt "each blow . . . might reach the cell and lance the heart of him who was to be the chief actor," but his brother-in-law reassured him that the condemned man would be sleeping soundly; "They always do!" The novelist was alert and excited, "somewhat painfully interested," Burnett remembered, "and taking mental notes." Then, looking into the crowd, Dickens suddenly exclaimed, "Why, there stands Thackeray!" At an impressive six foot three, Thackeray was quite a giant of a man, "like Saul, a head and shoulders higher than the filthy crowd," Burnett recalled. "Nobody who knew him could mistake him for any other." But though they called down to get his attention, it seemed that even if Thackeray had heard them, he would not have been able to move from the position he was in, "the people wedged him in so tightly." What was he doing among the "ruffians"? Dickens wondered.

"You must not think me inhospitable in refusing to sit up," Thackeray had written to Milnes the day before, forgoing the MP's invitation to join him at his club for the all-night party on 5 July; "I must go to bed, that's the fact, or I never shall be able to attend to the work of tomorrow properly." Thackeray was so keen that they should all get some sleep that he even offered Milnes a sofa, but, as it turned out, Thackeray was the sleepless one, kept wide awake all night by thoughts of what torments the condemned man must be suffering in his cell: "The light coming through the cell-window turns the gaoler's candle pale. Four hours more! . . . I heard all the clocks in the neighbourhood chime the hours in succession."

So when Milnes's smart carriage drew up outside 13 Great
Coram Street at three in the morning, and several tipsy men
staggered in for a pre-dawn breakfast of cold fowl and sherry,
Thackeray was quite haggard, but Milnes and his friends
were cheerful and excited, and keen to repeat all the ghoulish
jokes that had occurred to them earlier. "It is curious that a
murder is a great inspirer of jokes," Thackeray mused: "there
is a perpetual jingling antithesis between life and death, that
is sure of its effect."

Milnes's coachman had nodded off while the gentlemen
were breakfasting, and started from his sleep as the front door
shut behind them. The early morning streets seemed clean
and fresh, and the trees in the squares between Bloomsbury
and Snow Hill were full of midsummer verdure, with dew on
the grass in the gardens of Gray's Inn. As they drew nearer
to the prison, the amount of foot-traffic increased dramatically; twice as many people, Thackeray imagined, as you'd
usually see on a busy street at midday. Some of the gin shops
had opened early, and the atmosphere was already lively and
anticipatory, as Thackeray described it in the extraordinary
essay he wrote two weeks later, "Going to See a Man Hanged":
"Many young dandies are there with moustaches and cigars;
some quiet fat family-parties, of simple honest tradesmen and
their wives, as we fancy, who are looking on with the greatest
imaginable calmness, and sipping their tea."

But, turning into the street where the scaffold had been set
up, there was "a kind of dumb electric shock" as the gallows
came into view: "There it stands, black and ready, jutting out
from a little door in the prison." Thackeray noted how the
windows of the houses opposite were crowded with onlookers, and that seats had even been put out on the rooftops to
form extra viewing space. This paying crowd was full of tipsy,

dissolute young men, slatternly women "giggling, drinking
and romping" and a disturbing number of young girls, he reported, adding, as an irresistible dig at Dickens, "some that
Cruikshank and Boz might have taken as a study for Nancy."
He had no idea that Dickens himself was in one of those windows, looking down. There were plenty of "blackguards and
boys" too, up near the front of the crowd, "stunted, sallow,
ill-grown lads, in ragged fustian, scowling about"—a marked
contrast to the tall, well-fed and smartly dressed policemen
who defended the barrier between them and the scaffold.

The extraordinary social mix at the execution also included plenty of representatives of the upper classes, 600 of
whom had tickets to observe the hanging from inside the gaol.
Outside, in the most expensive windows, could be seen (and
heard) the clubmen and sportsmen, "aristocratic brutes . . .
who must have *excitement* of one sort or another," as the
Hampshire Independent reported with deep disapproval, and
even some "elegantly-dressed females" who were preparing
to watch the proceedings through their opera glasses. "They
wished to know if [the condemned man] was (in cant phrase)
'*game to the last*'" (like Jack Sheppard), the paper lamented.
"Why, is not this the way to encourage murder, is it not giving '*ton*' to blood and crime?" To drive the point home, they
decided to name and shame some of the aristocrats present:
Lord Lowth, Lord Glentworth, Lord Alfred Paget and Count
d'Orsay.

Forty thousand people was a lot of London, at a time when
the total population of the city was under two million.* Who
else was present in the crowd that morning besides d'Orsay,

---

* The 1841 census recorded 1,945,000 people in the capital.

Dickens, Thackeray, Burnett, Maclise, Fred Dickens, Monckton Milnes and his club friends? It seems likely that many of the Metropolitan Police officers who had taken part in the Lord William Russell murder case would have had a professional and personal curiosity in seeing the thing through, but what of Mr. Cummings, for instance, who had conveyed the stolen cutlery to court, or that host of Soho workers who testified in various capacities at the trial: the print-seller, the washerwoman, the aurist? Was Madame Piolaine there, treating Louis Gardie and Joseph Vincent to a drink from her £50 reward?

The *Era* reported there being a high number of menservants at the execution, "evincing the fearful interest taken in the culprit's fate by the class to which he had belonged," but what of the other servants who had known him on Norfolk Street—Daniel Young, Thomas Selway, William York and George Doubleday—his colleagues from Fector's and from Lady Julia Lockwood's household, including his friends the Pethouds? Or Mr. Fector himself, once so keen to intervene in the valet's defence? Would Courvoisier's uncle Louis have been there, praying fervently for his nephew, or the aunt who had imagined him soon entering a better world? It would surely have been too distressing to witness. Likewise, would Sarah Mancer and Mary Hannell have stayed away, though so many others did not?

One person who is almost certain to have been watching was Henry Carr. He was Courvoisier's oldest and best friend in England, and their dealings around the time of the murder had all the marks of a continuing close association. If Courvoisier had a collaborator, Carr is the most obvious candidate, and even if the valet had said nothing about his immediate plans to his friend, his general ambition to better his lot in life by means of petty crime must have been known by Carr, and possibly shared.

And it is hard to think of Henry Carr staying away from Newgate that morning on grounds of delicacy. As Dickens said six years later in his reflections on the subject, there is a "horrible fascination" about the punishment of death, "which, in the minds—not of evil-disposed persons, but of good and virtuous and well-conducted people, supersedes the horror legitimately attaching to crime itself." This "attraction of repulsion" was "generally speaking, irresistible . . . being as much a law of our moral nature, as gravitation is in the structure of the visible world."

Courvoisier had been watched carefully by the turnkeys as he tried to take his last few fitful hours of sleep. He asked to be woken at 4 a.m. in order to write some final messages to his family and friends, and was said to be very busy doing so, though none of those letters has survived. At 7:30, he received the sacrament from Mr. Baup, who stayed with him all the way to the scaffold. Then the sheriffs procured some books for him to sign, as soon-to-be valuable souvenirs, a ghastly reminder of his useless fame: "The 6th of July, 1840, the day of my execution," he wrote in one. Thomas Calcraft, the hangman, arrived promptly at 7:50, with a rope in a bag. Courvoisier's hands were tied together at the front, the knell tolled and the procession began along the dark prison corridors, the chaplain walking ahead and reading the burial service as they went.

The actor Charles Kean was one of the 600 "noblemen and gentlemen" who had been given privileged access to the gaol by the prison authorities to observe the prisoner's final prayers and the procession to the scaffold. Kean was there in a semi-professional capacity, hoping to glean insights for his craft from the extraordinary situation of the prisoner; his father, Edmund Kean, had once done the same by witnessing the execution of the Cato Street ringleader, Arthur Thistlewood. But Kean can hardly have been prepared for the sort of behaviour he saw in the passageways of Newgate that morning. As soon as Courvoisier appeared, there was a rush among the visitors, not aggressive so much as enthusiastic, and despite his best attempts, Cope and his men couldn't keep them at bay. They all seemed to want to get as near Courvoisier as possible and "the greatest confusion" was created in the narrow doorways as they tried to squeeze through at once. Cries of "Shame, shame!" didn't stop anyone.

This scrum was going on as the death-bell began to toll from St. Sepulchre's, when the atmosphere in the crowd outside changed instantly. Heads were uncovered and a "great murmur" of dreadful anticipation went round, "more awful, *bizarre*, and indescribable than any sound I had ever heard before," Thackeray wrote. "Women and children began to shriek horribly. I don't know if it was the bell I heard; but a dreadful quick feverish kind of jangling noise mingled with the noise of the people, and lasted for about two minutes. The scaffold stood before us, tenantless and black; the black chain was hanging down ready from the beam. Nobody came." Whispers went round that the condemned man had been reprieved—or that he had killed himself. Then the door opened and the small procession appeared. " 'That's he—that's he!' you heard the people say, as the devoted man came up."

So Courvoisier appeared in front of the ocean of faces, in a new black suit, hands tied in front of him. He walked firmly, but looked around distractedly. "He opened his hands in a helpless kind of way," Thackeray noticed, "and clasped them once or twice together. He turned his head here and there, and looked about him for an instant with a wild imploring look. His mouth was contracted into a sort of pitiful smile." When he went to place himself under the beam, with his face towards the chapel, the hangman turned him round the other way. Perhaps there was a difference in prices between the rooms the victim faced and those from which his face was hidden.

The unearthly yells and groans which rose from the crowd continued all through the execution, and when Calcraft pulled the hood over Courvoisier's face, Thackeray could look no more: "I am not ashamed to say that I shut my eyes as the last dreadful act was going on which sent this wretched guilty soul into the presence of God." The newspapers were less squeamish, and reported how rapidly the hanging commenced, and how long it went on: "The moment the rope was suspended to the beam, the bolt was drawn, and in about a minute and a half this miserable man ceased to exist." *A minute and a half.*

The spectacle over and body removed back into the gaol, the vast crowd slowly began to move again and break up. There was a paragraph in one of the papers on 11 July in which the police and Newgate authorities were congratulated for having managed the event so peaceably: 40,000 people gathered in one place without a single accident! But another paper contradicted this flatly, saying that at the moment when the bolt on the drop was pulled, someone from a gang of thieves operating among the crowd in Giltspur Street caused a panic by shouting "Mad bull!" and "many hundreds were thrown to the ground, persons standing in light carts were overturned, and very considerable mischief and serious accidents occurred." According to this account, many of the erstwhile hanging-watchers ended up being taken to St. Bartholomew's hospital with broken bones.

Dickens made prompt use of his observations on that dismal morning, putting the details of the execution straight into the climax of *Barnaby Rudge*, where Barnaby's father and his co-conspirator are hanged outside Newgate: "All was brightness and promise, excepting the street below into which the eye looked down as into a dark trench, where, in the midst of so much life, and hope, and renewal of existence, stood the terrible instrument of death." The nooses "dangling in the light like loathsome garlands" make an obscene but riveting sight, and "even little children were held up above the people's heads to see what kind of a toy a gallows was, and learn how men were hanged." "It was terrible to see," Barnaby relates, "the world of eager eyes, all strained upon the scaffold and the beam."

The novelist in Dickens readily saw what to make of Courvoisier's execution, while the social reformer in him had a slightly different agenda. Six years after the occasion, he wrote about his personal feelings that day in a series of letters to the *Daily News* on the subject of capital punishment, calling for reform of the law. Revulsion at the spectacle of seeing a man hanged had been gaining ground for some time, and juries increasingly often chose verdicts of "insanity" when they couldn't face sending a murderer to his death, so Dickens was more of an influencer than an initiator in this campaign (Milnes did far more). But his eloquence and, by 1846, his standing in the public eye gave significant weight to Dickens's memories of Courvoisier's death and his rousing denunciation of the dehumanizing effects of watching it:

From the moment of my arrival, when there were but a few score boys in the street, and all those young thieves, and all clustered together behind the barrier nearest to the drop—down to the time when I saw the body with its dangling head, being carried on a wooden bier into the gaol—I did not see one token in all the immense crowd; at the windows, in the streets, on the house-tops, anywhere; of any one emotion suitable to the occasion. No sorrow, no salutary terror, no abhorrence, no seriousness; nothing but ribaldry, debauchery, levity, drunkenness and flaunting vice in fifty other shapes. I should have deemed it impossible that I could have ever felt any large assemblage of my fellow-creatures to be so odious. I hoped, for an instant, that there was some sense of Death and Eternity in the cry of "Hats Off!" when the miserable wretch appeared, but I found, next moment, that they only raised it as they would at a Play—to see the Stage the better, in the final scene.

If Dickens had wished to see someone filled with some "emotion suitable to the occasion," he needed only to have looked at Thackeray. Thackeray also compared the scene to being in the pit at a play, with the people around him chatting to one another in an anticipatory way and passing the time in jokes and animated commentary. Only a small minority of them were drunks and riff-raff, he thought, and where Dickens interpreted the baring of heads as a ghoulish practicality, Thackeray took it as the conventional sign of respect. Unlike Dickens and Burnett, he was struck by the essential decency of the people around him—perhaps because he was standing among them.

It wasn't the crowd who disgusted Thackeray so much as the sickening practice he had witnessed. "I fully confess that I came away down Snow Hill that morning with a disgust for murder," he wrote, "but it was for the murder I saw done . . . It seems to me I have been abetting an act of frightful wickedness and violence, performed by a set of men against one of their fellows, and I pray God it may soon be out of the power of any man in England to witness such a hideous and degrading sight." As he and Milnes made their way back through the throng, they came across two little girls, aged about eleven and twelve, one of whom was crying to be taken away. They helped these children to safety out of the rush of bodies and asked what they were doing in such a place. "The child grinned knowingly, and said, 'We've koom to see the mon hanged!' Tender law, that brings out babes upon such errands, and provides them with such gratifying moral spectacles!"

The Dickens group also came away from Newgate in a sombre mood. "A ghastly night in Hades" is how Burnett described his unwanted experience later: the leering crowds, the appalling high tide of excitement, the noise, the crush, the dreadful finale of the drop. He and Dickens and Maclise all agreed that though they hated the murderer, they hated the punishment more, and if any of them had been able to save Courvoisier, he would have done it. "It was so loathsome, pitiful and vile a sight," Dickens remarked, "that the law appeared to be as bad as he."

As soon as Courvoisier's body was carried into the gaol, someone from Madame Tussaud's waxworks exhibition was let into the room where it lay to make a death mask. With this, and the sketches taken in court, they would quickly have a lifelike effigy of the murderer on display; sometimes it took only a day or two to get a model on show. Business was brisk in other souvenirs of the occasion: a ballad about the execution, illustrated with a crude generic woodcut of a hanging man, was already on sale to as many of the vast execution crowd as the printer could cater for. "The Lament of François Courvoisier" (to be sung, inappropriately enough, to the tune of "The Bank of Primroses") gives this warning résumé of the murderer's road to ruin:

> I was brought up by honest Parents:
> In Switzerland I first drew my breath,
> And now, for the horrid crime of murder
> I am doomed to meet an ignominious death.

One of the literati notably absent from the watchers that day was William Harrison Ainsworth, but if Ainsworth had hoped that the drop would prove the end of his association with this notorious crime, he was mistaken, for "The Lament" went on to pin the blame for Courvoisier's corruption wholly and solely at the feet of the bestselling story:

> To the Surrey for to see Jack Sheppard
> To beguile the time I went one night,
> But I little thought, that fateful evening
> That it would all my fair prospects blight.

> Alas! that night has proved my ruin;
> In innocent blood I have my hands imbrued,
> I was unworthy of such a master
> Who to me was always kind and good.

The public houses around Newgate were full all that day; no one seemed eager to get away from the scene of the execution, and some who had not been able to get near earlier now came to view the site, as a journalist who stayed around to get material for his sketch reported: "Even at three o'clock in the afternoon . . . the shed in which the apparatus of death is kept continued to be the mark of eager eyes." People were squinting through the keyhole and gaps in the planks of this structure to see the dark shape of the gibbet inside, with some of the prisoner's discarded clothes and a quart pot next to it. A group of boys, "mere children," as the journalist noted, were cracking jokes about these items and chalking up "uncouth representations of the morning's work" on the pavement and walls. "Here again was the morality of public death made obvious," he remarked disapprovingly.

There was no comfort for Ainsworth here either, for in his description of this post-mortem scene, the journalist happens to mention the tune these urchins were singing as they laughed and joked over their chalk pictures of the valet's death. It was *Jack Sheppard*'s theme, the summer's inescapable song, penned by Ainsworth with such pride and brio back in 1834, and now the sardonic soundtrack to a public execution: "Nix My Dolly, Pals, Fake Away."

9

The Aftermath

THACKERAY TOOK A LONG TIME TO RECOVER FROM THE trauma of Courvoisier's execution, writing to his mother that he had "the blue devils" for a fortnight afterwards, and couldn't dismiss from his mind the sight of Courvoisier on the scaffold: "I can't do my work and yet work must be done for the poor babbies' sake. It is most curious the effect his death has had on me, and I am trying to work it off in a paper on the subject. Meanwhile it weighs upon the mind, like cold plum pudding on the stomach, & as soon as I begin to write, I get melancholy."

Thackeray now felt ashamed and degraded by the curiosity which had taken him to Newgate, yet the spectacle of the execution (that he didn't actually watch to the end) had opened his eyes in another way, moving him to change the "pleasant piece" he had intended to write for *Blackwood's* into the emotionally charged essay "Going to See a Man Hanged" which *Fraser's* published in August. What does the spectacle of a public execution achieve, he asked, and what does it do to the people watching? Why does anyone—let alone 40,000 people—choose to go there in the first place? Thackeray made his piece deliberately personal, discarding what he called "the magazine 'We,'" in order to speak face to face with the reader, "recording every one of the impressions felt by him as honestly as he could"—an innovative form of journalism. The shame that he felt watching the hanging had surprised the author, but that was nothing to the horror of it: "The whole of the sickening, ghastly, wicked scene passes before the eyes again; and indeed it is an awful one to see, and very hard and painful to describe."

> . . . on a Monday morning, at eight o'clock, this man is placed under a beam, with a rope connecting it and him; a plank disappears from under him, and those who have paid for good places may see the hands of the Government agent, Jack Ketch, coming up from his black hole, and seizing the prisoner's legs, and pulling them, until he is quite dead—strangled.

It was incalculably bad for people to witness such things, Thackeray argued, just as it was bad for their worst tastes and instincts to be pandered to, but, like the little girls who had "koom to see the mon hanged!," few could resist such a show.

> This is the 20th of July, and I may be permitted for my part to declare that, for the last fourteen days, so salutary has the impression of the butchery been upon me, I have had the man's face continually before my eyes; that I can see Mr. Ketch at this moment, with an easy air, taking the rope from his pocket; that I feel myself ashamed and degraded at the brutal curiosity which took me to that brutal sight; and that I pray to Almighty God to cause this disgraceful sin to pass from among us, and to cleanse our land of blood.

Madame Tussaud made a waxwork from the plaster death mask of Courvoisier and exhibited an effigy of him promptly, alongside ones of the contemporary murderers James Green-acre, Richard Gould and Dennis Collins, arranged together in a pretend dock. Her exhibition was doing well that year; many people wanted to come and see the model of the Queen, a portrait of whom appeared on the cover of the 1840 catalogue. Item number 15 was the errant servant:

> F. B. Courvoisier, Taken from Life, and from his Mask after Death . . . the horrid murderer of Lord William Russell, in the 72nd year of his age, with whom he lived as valet. Courvoisier was born in Switzerland, and passed many years in England. He was executed on the 6th of July.

In later years, Tussaud's showed a gruesomely lifelike model of Courvoisier's head, with hair and colouring added, and eyes closed, in the collection that became the Chamber of Horrors, and it was still there, under a glass cover, well into the twentieth century.* Cruder waxwork figures of the murderer abounded in travelling shows and local fairs that year, though one, at a booth in Wincanton in Somerset, came to a violent end when a local man, told the figure was meant to represent Courvoisier, knocked its head off, saying such a person was not welcome in their town. He was later charged 10s 6d in damages.

The murderer's head was also the first subject in a

---

* The whereabouts of this effigy are currently unknown, and it may have been destroyed in a fire at Tussaud's warehouse in the 1970s. Some unpleasant photographs of it remain, though.

new series of monographs, *Illustrations of Phrenology*, that appeared the following year, written by Dickens's friend John Elliotson. Illustrations from three angles accompanied the text; it was a large and "powerful" specimen, Elliotson commented, twenty-three and a half inches in circumference, but oddly shaped: narrow at the forehead, rising to a larger back and sides. There were large measurements in areas associated with sexual love, self-esteem, cautiousness, violence, cunning and "Love of Notice," but benevolence scored low, as did wit and "Higher Intellectual Faculties," and the bulging back of the skull showed a brutishly large capacity for "General Observation" and "Sense of Things." All in all, Courvoisier presented one of the worst cerebral developments the phrenologist had ever seen.

Casts of the head were available from various suppliers, Elliotson informed readers; he preferred the one he had bought at Donovan's, which was "more accurate than that at Delville's, from having been taken after the swelling caused by the execution had subsided."

Little discussion of the case itself continued after the execution, and the police dealt privately with an enquiry into the behaviour of their officers at Norfolk Street during the searching of the house. Inspector Beresford and Constable Cronin were both exonerated by testimony from the workmen employed in dismantling the drains and chimneys; these witnesses asserted that the valet was kept under surveillance too close to allow him to hide all the objects he claimed in those days, and that he couldn't have kept the watch or locket as long as he said, as Inspector Tedman made him turn all his pockets out, and undo his shirt and waistcoat on the very first day of the investigation. As for the issue of the bloodstained gloves, the handkerchiefs and shirt front, it was felt that no further questions needed to be asked about this, though one officer (unnamed, but presumably Tedman) was severely reprimanded for negligence, and two constables were dismissed from their jobs. An argument was made in the press that if the police had planted those pieces of evidence, the items would surely have looked more decisively bloody, but whether this was meant seriously or satirically is hard to tell. Courvoisier's lately confessed penchant for lying meant that all such unresolved questions could now be laid at the door of his omissions or falsifications.

Sometime after the execution, a paragraph appeared in the papers, finally detailing the distribution of the £400 reward money "for the apprehension of the perpetrator or perpetrators of the diabolical deed." In acknowledgement of her pivotal witness to what had occurred in Norfolk Street, and perhaps also in compensation for the distress caused by the imputations to her character in the process, Sarah Mancer received £30, about a year's salary for a housemaid, and Mary Hannell got £10. The different sums given out among the police were less easy to account for, though, since Inspectors Beresford and Tedman were each awarded £60, but Inspector Pearce received £100. The remaining £140 was distributed among the constables who served in the case (excluding the sacked ones) and James Ellis, Lord William's former valet. "It is somewhat difficult to imagine why Inspector Pearce should have had a larger amount awarded to him than Tedman," one paper remarked; Tedman had, after all, been the first to take Courvoisier into custody, and his conduct throughout the case was specifically praised by the judge. But presumably the lower figure reflected his failure to stop people getting at the suspect's box and possibly Pearce's generous bonus was connected in some way with exposing that, as well as his sharp-eyed spotting of the loose skirting board.

Criticism of Charles Phillips built up after the trial, stoked not just by the letters of "Manlius" to the *Morning Chronicle* but by bad coverage in the press generally, especially the Sunday papers (always the most lurid of the week), which accused the barrister of profanity for saying, "The omniscient God alone knew who did the crime." Phillips, fearing that such publicity might be detrimental to his standing at the bar, went to Judges Tindall and Parke for corroboration that those had not been his *exact* words, but the damage was done. The *Examiner* made his conduct of the defence the focus of several articles that week, including the lead, calling for a change in the criminal law: "Whether [Phillips's behaviour] accords or not with professional morality, it is not for us to decide; but if it does, the public will probably be disposed to think that the profession should change its name from the profession of the Law to the profession of the Lie." Phillips, they claimed, was little better than an accomplice after the fact.

Phillips's defence of Courvoisier remained a target for more than a decade. Dickens brought it up in letters to the *Daily News* in 1846 and to *The Times* in 1849, when another very high-profile murder case, the trial of Frederick and Maria Manning for the murder of her lover, brought the Courvoisier trial back to mind, not least because Maria Manning was also a Swiss servant. Wilkins, the prosecuting counsel in the Manning case, was heavily criticized for his conduct, but the *Examiner* used it as an occasion to note some "progress of opinion" in the intervening nine years: "How much worse was Mr. Phillips's attempt to throw the suspicion of the murder of Lord William Russell on the innocent female servants, in order to procure the acquittal of his client Courvoisier, of whose guilt he was cognizant!" Phillips had been promoted soon after, while the servant . . . what had happened to her?

The answer was that Sarah Mancer had fallen on very hard times indeed. She suffered a nervous collapse as a result of the murder and its consequences, and found it impossible to get another job. The much-deserved £30 reward cannot have lasted her long. Presently, the following advert appeared in the press:

> SARAH MANCER, the housemaid to the late Lord William Russell—The persecution this poor woman underwent, the harassing interrogations to which she was subjected preceding the providential discovery of the guilt of Courvoisier, have so prostrated her mental faculties and bodily strength, as to unfit her for those duties her station in life have called her to. Some persons have, therefore, ventured this appeal to public charity, for the purpose of raising a fund to be applied in alleviation of her present and future wants.

The identities of the concerned persons who made this charitable initiative aren't known; unlike Courvoisier, Sarah Mancer had not gained any influential friends during her ordeal. The lawyer Francis Hobler wrote bitterly of the Russell family's later negligence of the servants involved in the case; all of them were out of work for a long time, and though Mary Hannell and William York finally found jobs, George Doubleday did not, and became destitute. Hobler believed that if John Tedman hadn't known this, and, out of charity, kept an eye on him and "relieved [him] with food" from time to time, Doubleday would certainly have starved.

The family did nothing for Sarah Mancer, even though she was too ill to work, and some months after the advertisement a further notice regretfully announced that the subscription had been a failure and was being wound up. Within a few years, Mancer was reported to have been consigned to a pauper lunatic asylum, possibly the worst of all Victorian institutions, where, sometime in the later 1840s, she eventually died.

Richard Monckton Milnes rode home from Newgate on 6 July in a much less perturbed state of mind than his friend Thackeray. "A man of the world by profession," as Henry Adams once called him, he had got what he set out for—information—and employed it in his vigorous campaigns for reform to the law on capital punishment. He spoke on the subject frequently in Parliament in the coming years and was the moving force behind a Royal Commission on Capital Punishment a decade later, paving the way for the legislation which eventually put an end to public executions. Dickens, not Thackeray, became the figurehead of this campaign, and his letters on capital punishment to *The Times* at the time of the Mannings' execution in 1849 (which he also witnessed) had considerable weight. "I am solemnly convinced," Dickens said, "that nothing that ingenuity could devise to be done in this city, in the same compass of time, could work such ruin as one public execution, and I stand astounded and appalled by the wickedness it exhibits."

Dickens wrote to *The Times* again a few days later, questioning whether public hanging had any deterrent effect at all, or in fact did harm to its observers (which had been Thackeray's thought too). He came to think that the publicity given to the perpetrators of crime was an evil in itself and suggested that there should be a complete shutdown of contact with the outside world after a sentence of death; no visitors, no printed confessions or turnkey reports, "his sayings and doings being served up in print on Sunday mornings for the perusal of families." The execution should be private, solemn and attended only by prison officials and perhaps a "witness jury" of twenty-four people (i.e., white men), eight from each of three strata, "low," "higher" and "higher still," "so that it might fairly represent all classes of society."

The law did change, eventually: capital punishment continued, but after 1868 all executions were conducted within the walls of the prison, witnessed only by officials. Edward Bulwer, now Baron Bulwer-Lytton and a member of the House of Lords, was not slow to take some of the credit, going as far as to say that his previously reviled novel *Paul Clifford* had significantly influenced "the wise and great relaxation of our criminal code," "for it is not till art has told the unthinking that nothing (*rightly treated*) is too low for its breath to vivify, and its wings to raise, that the herd awaken from their chronic lethargy of contempt, and the lawgiver is compelled to redress what the poet has lifted into esteem." A grandiose reading of the case, perhaps, but slightly forgivable, given the amount of criticism his book had received in the past.

Dickens was finally able to finish *Barnaby Rudge* in the second half of 1840, and get Newgate out of his system. He had been keen to dissociate himself from the "felon literature" controversy all year, and specifically from the accusations Thackeray had levelled at him in *Catherine*. In a reprint of *Oliver Twist* published in the year after Lord William's murder, Dickens claimed that his novel was much more in the tradition of Fielding and Defoe than Bulwer and Ainsworth, and had done exactly what Thackeray said he had failed signally to do, "show [criminals] as they really are, for ever skulking uneasily through the dirtiest paths of life, with the great, black ghastly gallows closing up their prospect, turn them where they may." "It appeared to me," he continued, bullishly, "that to do this, would be to attempt a something which was greatly needed, and which would be a service to society." The writers who deserved to be vilified on this score were the out-and-out romancers, who beguiled readers with "canterings upon moonlit heaths [and] merry-makings in the snuggest of all possible caverns"—Ainsworth and Bulwer, that is. Dickens remained sensitive on the subject and kept adjusting the text of *Oliver Twist* in successive editions to make it look less "Newgate." And perhaps more telling, from the point of view of the change in his feelings towards Ainsworth, was a much less noticeable bit of editing, when he removed the footnote praising the author of *Rookwood* from later editions of his first book, *Sketches by Boz*.

Following Courvoisier's execution, there were moves to suppress the influence of the book and play which had done so much to "familiarize the imagination with deeds of blood, and to hold up to admiration the savage criminals acting in them," as Sheriff Evans had said. It began with a two-decade-long ban by the Lord Chamberlain on the play of *Jack Sheppard*,* and warnings about the book's influence appearing in a House of Commons enquiry into the employment of children, "and on their physical, intellectual, and moral character," in which the commissioners bemoaned the ignorance of the rising generation: "They know nothing, except what is calculated to deprave them, and though few have ever

---

* This ban was circumvented with ease by determined producers, who simply changed the titles of their plays.

heard of Moses or Christ—or even Wellington or Nelson—
they mostly all know something about Dick Turpin, and Jack
Sheppard the robber and prison breaker." But the Jack Sheppard craze had a life of its own and what had been solely a
London phenomenon in the winter of 1839 had soon spread
to the provinces. Two years after the first wave of copycat
criminals had shocked the capital, an even more damning report on delinquency in Liverpool showed an extraordinary
number of cases connecting crimes with having seen the play.
The Liverpool youths admitted that they would steal to get to
see *Jack Sheppard* and typically went a number of times; no
wonder the journalist commenting on the statistics in *Chambers's Edinburgh Journal* lamented the unflagging popularity
of "felon literature" and "the deification of great thieves by
thoughtless novelists." His harsh conclusion was that "men
able and willing to become the authors of such fictions, are
more dangerous public enemies than it is possible for any
other class of private citizens to be."

The long controversy about *Jack Sheppard* did Ainsworth
real damage. After Courvoisier's confessions, he was black-
balled at the Trinity Club, and to add insult to injury, heard
the news by letter from the man who had done more than anyone to shoot his novel down, John Forster: "I regret much, my
dear W.H.A., to be obliged to communicate to you the forego-
ing resolution . . ." The Countess of Blessington jumped to her
friend's support, offering to exert her influence to get Ainsworth into the Athenaeum instead, but he declined, partly
out of pride and partly from practicality; the novelist had
heard that he would get a cold welcome there, "having been
given to understand that I should meet with formidable
opposition from a hostile party, whom I must term the Anti-
Jack-Sheppardites."

Even his formerly close friends, such as Dickens, had started to worry about books "after Mr. Ainsworth's fashion." Richard Bentley, his publisher and proprietor of the magazine which had serialized *Jack Sheppard*, suddenly lost faith in him and quarrelled with Ainsworth bitterly, as a result of which the novelist and his illustrator Cruikshank left and set up the defiantly titled *Ainsworth's Magazine* (not half so successful). Ainsworth continued to write prolifically and profitably, but he never again chose a story with a criminal hero and after *Jack Sheppard* his great fame was over. When John Forster mentioned Ainsworth's name in a letter of the 1860s, Robert Browning replied, "Good heavens! Is he still alive?"

Ten years later, there was still a shadow around his book and unfinished business connected with the "Anti-Jack-Sheppardites." Grateful for a good notice of a new edition of the novel, Ainsworth wrote to the reviewer, Charles Kent, "I did intend to introduce the republication of this much maligned romance with some prefatory remarks, but I could not have done so without offence to some persons, who, to serve their own purposes, got up a 'cry' against me . . . It required some forbearance to let the occasion pass, especially as I am sure I could make my case good, for I really believe the romance to be harmless—as harmless at least as *Oliver Twist* and *Paul Clifford*." Unlike Dickens, who kept tinkering with *Oliver Twist*, he had made no changes to *Jack Sheppard*, and stood by his work, though by 1850 the historical novel was out of fashion and getting a decidedly bad press. Novels of "issues" had become much more acceptable, critically— Fanny Trollope's *Life and Adventures of Michael Armstrong, the Factory Boy*, Benjamin Disraeli's *Sybil*, Elizabeth Gaskell's *Mary Barton*, for example—and that was the direction in which Dickens was heading too, with *Nicholas Nickleby* and, later, *Bleak House* and *Hard Times*. Sensational stories were increasingly wrapped up in "puzzle" plots, which promised some gentle intellectual exercise for readers to justify any rude excitements, and the sudden rise and fall of "criminal romance" looks in retrospect like the pivot around which this change took place; as newspapers took over the explicit reporting of crime and punishment, such literature became gentrified, in the form of the detective novel.

One of the great proponents of the new type of fiction was Dickens's American admirer and Ainsworth's detractor, Edgar Allan Poe. Poe studied *Barnaby Rudge* as it appeared in monthly instalments in 1841 and was fascinated by the mechanics of the mystery, correctly guessing long before the serialization was complete that Barnaby was the murderer's son. He was particularly taken by the use of the raven in the story, but thought more could have been done with it. "Intensely amusing as it is," he wrote in a review of the book, "[the raven] might have been made, more than we now see it, a portion of the conception of the fantastic Barnaby. Its croakings might have been *prophetically* heard." When Dickens was visiting Philadelphia in 1842, Poe wrote requesting an interview, sending along his articles on Dickens's work and a copy of *Tales of the Grotesque and Arabesque* to establish his suitability; the novelist duly met him twice and was impressed.

It's hard to imagine that Grip didn't enter their conversations. The original bird was dead by this time,* but Dickens had had him stuffed and mounted in a glass case in his study, where he stayed until the novelist's death in 1870. Poe, mean-

---

* The first Grip, that is; Dickens got a replacement later, and named him the same.

while, saw through his idea of a prophetically croaking bird with extravagant aplomb in his poem "The Raven," which was to become his best-known, best-loved work:

> Once upon a midnight dreary, while I pondered, weak
> and weary,
> Over many a quaint and curious volume of forgotten
> lore—
> While I nodded, nearly napping, suddenly there came
> a tapping,
> As of some one gently rapping, rapping at my
> chamber door.
> " 'Tis some visitor," I muttered, "tapping at my
> chamber door—
> Only this and nothing more."

The original Grip was sold at auction after Dickens's death, but, with a pleasing sort of circularity, a later collector of Dickens memorabilia who had acquired the bird appreciated the connection with Poe and bequeathed Grip to the Free Library of Philadelphia, where he remains, beak at the ready for interesting ankles, to this day.

Though he had distanced himself from the "Newgate" phenomenon, Dickens was as alert as anyone to its power, and in his late career, when his highly dramatic public readings from his novels became popular, "The Murder of Nancy" was the episode he performed most frequently. It became something of an obsession with him, and he threw himself into his impersonation of Bill Sikes with excessive zeal, bringing on a collapse after one performance in January 1870 that is thought to have hastened his death four months later. "My ordinary pulse is 72," he wrote to his friend Wills after the reading, "and it runs up under this effort to 112. Besides which, it takes me ten or twelve minutes to get my wind back at all." But Dickens was gripped by the most sensational scene of his most "Newgate" novel, drawn to its vitality and visceral appeal as ardently as anyone in the pit. Few writers of his age knew better what an audience wanted.

His attacks on Charles Phillips in the 1840s in the *Morning Chronicle* and the *Daily News* had been those of one public rhetorician to another, but there was another, much more personal reverberation from their antagonism, for in the 1850s Dickens's troublesome (married) younger brother Augustus ran away to America with Phillips's only daughter, Bertha. It was a "migratory divorce," in the terminology of the day, with Bertha assuming the name "Mrs. A. N. Dickens" on arrival in New York, and retaining it for the rest of her life. Although he was involved in a long-standing extramarital affair of his own (with the actress Ellen Ternan), Dickens disapproved harshly of his brother's behaviour, and avoided Chicago, where Augustus and Bertha had settled, on his future book tours, and made a point of sending money to Augustus's first wife and none to Bertha and her six children by Augustus after she was widowed, for which he came in for some criticism. But it was a story with a tragic ending, for Bertha became destitute and committed suicide in 1864.

Sarah Mancer was not the only person to be severely affected by the trauma of Lord William's death. Edwin Landseer's breakdown in May 1840 stopped him working for almost a year. His mother had died that winter, his widowed mistress, the former Duchess of Bedford, had refused to marry him and he had professional pressures, but it was the senseless slaughter of his old friend that seems to have tipped him over the edge. His close associations with the whole Russell family meant that he had been party to every detail of the unfolding story in Norfolk Street, and felt the shock of it profoundly. And in a small paragraph in *The Times* that summer was news of another sad outcome from the case. In the household of the Duchess of Argyll (second wife to the late Lady William Russell's former admirer, the Duke) the children's governess had apparently run mad, "excited after the murder of Lord William Russell," and had attempted to kill her mistress. The crazed woman's plan was thwarted by the intervention of the Duchess's stepdaughter Emma, and the governess was subsequently sent to an asylum, but it was a stark illustration of the lingering horror felt by people connected to the crime, as well as the apparent volatility of master–servant relations which it had stirred up.

The Courvoisier case did produce one very beneficial consequence, though it took fifty years to come to light. In among all the crank letters which the police and family received during the investigation was one written only ten days after the murder by a Norfolk surgeon called Robert Blake Overton. Having read in the papers that a single bloody handprint had been left on one of Lord William's bedsheets, Dr. Overton had an ingenious suggestion to make, for he had been doing some private study of handprints and wished, respectfully, to pass his findings on: "It is not generally known that every individual has a peculiar arrangement [on] the grain of the skin," he told Lord John Russell, to whom the letter was addressed, "[and] I would strongly recommend the propriety of obtaining impressions from the fingers of the suspected individual

and a comparison made with the marks on the sheets and pil-
lows." Nothing was done with this suggestion, though Lord
John passed it to Scotland Yard; by the time Overton wrote
his letter, much of the evidence, such as the mattresses and
sheets of Lord William's bed, had been destroyed, so perhaps
no bloody prints remained. It is also likely that the Home
Office thought Overton's theory far-fetched, even though
he illustrated it with examples of his own fingerprints and
those of another subject. Whatever the reason, his letter lay
unattended in Scotland Yard's files until the 1890s, when
someone, reading the old papers about the Courvoisier case,
thought to investigate this first intimation that there could be
such a thing as fingerprint identification. Belatedly, but spectacularly, Overton's idea took off. Had it been pursued in the
1840s, it is believed that many of the century's most notorious
crimes, such as the murders by "Jack the Ripper," could have
been solved.

And finally, what end for the man whose book had caused
such commotion, William Harrison Ainsworth? In a magazine profile of 1877 ("Celebrities at Home"), thirty-seven years
after the murder, he is described as being in surprisingly good
repair, living in a comfortable villa near Hurstpierpoint on
the South Downs, with his dashing portrait by Daniel Maclise
displayed prominently on the staircase, next to an execution-
er's axe and a sword. He had written twenty-five more novels
since the "nightmare" book, which he still insisted was perfectly moral: "I never had the remotest intention of holding
vice up to admiration in *Jack Sheppard*," he told his inter-
viewer. "If I have done so, I believe Hogarth to be equally
culpable." The fact is Ainsworth had always known he was

romanticizing his criminal heroes, and played up to it. At the end of *Rookwood*, he could not part without an envoi: "Oh rare Dick Turpin! Perhaps we have placed him in too favourable a point of view; and yet we know not . . ." One critic has called this a lack of "moral curiosity" on Ainsworth's part, something that Dickens had to excess. Perhaps an essential difference between the two writers lies there.

But at his villa, Little Rockley, in 1877, Ainsworth was unapologetic. "I plead guilty to the charge of Jacobitism," he said gaily to his visitor, as, hunting through his library, he called attention to several fine copies of Scott and Defoe and a first edition of Fielding's *Tom Jones;* "I am a Jacobite, and am proud of it." And as the journalist sat down with Ainsworth to a lunch of capons in egg sauce, washed down with a "sound" claret, he judged him still "full of life and spirit, and full of work."

As for *Jack Sheppard*, unlike *Oliver Twist*, Ainsworth's novel did not survive its season of hyper-celebrity, and perhaps was ultimately too badly written to last more than a generation. Even Forster ceased to attack it in the press, and by 1844 Elizabeth Barrett's correspondent and admirer Richard Horne was able to write the obituary of the controversial bestseller: "*Jack Sheppard* did its evil work of popularity, and has now gone to its cradle in the cross-roads of literature."

Postscript: Unanswered Questions

FRANÇOIS BENJAMIN COURVOISIER TOOK THE BLAME FOR the murder of Lord William Russell, and died for it, but was this case ever truly solved? The drop put an end to speculation, but there still remain many unanswered questions.

It doesn't help that the person with the best knowledge of what happened in Norfolk Street on the night of 5th May 1840 was, by his own admission, an inveterate liar, but the amount of lying Courvoisier did, and the number of variations he proposed on the story of his crime, might tell us something in itself.

Courvoisier's own statements about his motives are very unconvincing. A murderous animus towards Lord William rings false: in the five weeks he worked for him, Courvoisier hadn't really had time to develop any real animus against his new employer, who was an unobjectionable old cove anyway—and Courvoisier himself eventually dismissed this as a reasonable claim. The motive given in his "official" confession seems feebler still: "I began two or three times not to like the place, I didn't know what to do[,] I thought if I gave warning none of my friends would take notice of me again, and I thought by making it appear a kind of robbery he would discharge me." How likely is it that a valet could be moved to kill his master through anxiety about what his friends would think if he didn't stay long in the job, and the damage it might do to his prospects? These are not sufficient motives for murder.

None of Courvoisier's confessions entirely supplants the others, and none necessarily tells any truth at all. They might be read now as a melange of facts and fantasies, which don't clarify what happened so much as multiply the possible scenarios, and one has to conclude that this was Courvoisier's intention. He seems to have been protecting the true story, or reserving it, by raising weak alternatives. "When I find that the truth has been spoken I will then tell all I know about it," he had said to one of the police officers in the first week of the investigation, when he was still a free man, but that time never came. Was he covering up for someone? An accomplice who could yet evade detection, even if he had not? Does this explain why he was turning his head "here and there" as he mounted the scaffold, and looking about "with a wild imploring look," as Thackeray had noted, his mouth contracted into a pitiful smile?

Madame Piolaine is just one of several people who seem to have known more about the valet than she was prepared to tell. Charles Phillips can be criticized for his heavy-handed attempts at impugning the respectability of her hotel when he cross-examined her at Courvoisier's trial, but he can't be blamed for his suspicions of her generally; the peculiar timeliness of her appearance with a parcel of stolen silverware might have come under much greater scrutiny had the trial not already been well under way, and heading towards an acquittal for lack of solidly incriminating evidence. The discovery of the stolen plate did indeed seem like a providential sign. But Madame Piolaine's story about being barely aware of the crime in Norfolk Street, and not linking "Jean" (whom she had just re-encountered and who had prompted her to recall their connection) with the young French-speaking valet suspected of his master's murder, indicates a slowness of wit rather at variance with her subsequent behaviour. For, once she perceived a possible link, what did she do but send for a lawyer and witnesses before the package was opened? Clearly she expected the contents to be significant.

Or had she opened it already in private, resealed it and called in Cummings to give the whole operation an air of surprise?

The penny-dropping moment about the identity of "Jean" had come, Madame Piolaine said, on or near 18 June, when her cousin Joseph Vincent had pointed out the reward notice in "a French paper." The edition of the paper in question had been kept and was seen in court, but the *Caledonian Mercury* of 25 June 1840 is the only contemporary newspaper to identify it as the *Gazette des Tribunaux*, a Paris weekly devoted to serious journalism about court cases and jurisprudence. It was clearly a rather specialist title for an ex-pat subscriber in Leicester Square to choose, as it didn't cover general news, either in France or in England. What it did cover in detail, though, in the summer of 1840, was the murder of Lord William Russell. Even on the first Sunday after the crime, the *Gazette* had a long account of the inquest, focusing on the valet's evidence (translated into French) and mentioning both him and Henry Carr by name. It also gave notice of the reward, though not mentioning the amount offered: "Une récompense a été annoncée pour ceux qui mettront la justice sur la trace des auteurs de ce forfait." This was on 10 May, only a week after "Jean" had appeared with his parcel, and coverage of the case continued all through the next six weeks. So much for Madame's news blackout.

Were they in collusion, or was Madame simply interested in the £50 reward, and unwilling to admit that she'd had a very good idea who "Jean" was all along?[*] Her evidence tipped the balance against him, but even then Courvoisier kept up his character of being an injured party, and a good servant, retaining it right to the end—a rather remarkable feat, given that he was doomed. It was the one consistent thing in the whole investigation, his maintenance of an appearance of innocence, and insistence he had acted alone.

During his last days in Newgate, when the prisoner issued so many different accounts of his actions, *The Times* gave up on trying to make sense of them: "it seems pretty clear that no credit can be given to any statement which has hitherto been made by this wretched culprit, except as regards the fact of the murder itself; but it would be idle to speculate on the motives of a mind so manifestly perverted." But, on the contrary, a little further speculation on his motives changes the look of this crime rather dramatically.

The prison chaplain, Mr. Carver, articulated the accepted view that the servant's hand had been raised "against a venerable and noble master, paltry consideration of money the base and only inducement—no provocation on the one hand—no necessity on the other—a good, an aged, a confiding master, brutally murdered in his sleep!" "Paltry" was right; it wasn't a botched burglary so much as an insignificant one, as Sir Harry Poland remarked in his edition of the trial

---

[*] She seems not to have shared the £50 (and another £20 which Lord John Russell gave her) with her husband Louis, who was sent to prison the following year as an insolvent, forced there by his partner, Joseph Vincent.

papers, published seventy-eight years after the event: "It is indeed shocking to think that this murder was committed by Courvoisier with the sole object of enabling him to steal a few pounds' worth of property with impunity." People were left to conclude that Courvoisier had had no real motive, but was purely bad. Does this explain the condemned man's emphasis on the influence of *Jack Sheppard* so late in the proceedings, to explain his corruption? Everyone was already convinced of the book's pernicious influence.

John Adolphus had warned the jury at Courvoisier's trial that the absence of an apparent motive was "a very erroneous test by which to judge of a man's innocence. They were not able to know the motives and impulses which led men to commit crime, and some offences of the greatest importance to society occurred, though no definite or rational motive could be discovered," he said, citing a "recent event" (Edward Oxford's attempted assassination of the Queen) to make his point; "neither man, nor prophet, nor even angel could tell the motive that induced it, and still it had been done." A killer, in other words, might always simply be a psychopath.

But Charles Phillips argued entirely from the opposite point of view, saying that "the most trifling action of human life had its spring from some motive or other." He listed the usual ones—hatred, jealousy, revenge, avarice, plunder—and ruled them out one by one: Lord William was a kind master who had trusted Courvoisier with all the duties of "a confidential servant" (including dressing and putting him to bed); where was any sign of hatred or jealousy? Revenge he also dismissed, and on the subject of plunder made the strong point that had Courvoisier been bent on thieving from Lord William, he had ample opportunity every day and did not need to stage a diverting break-in, still less murder his master and stay on the premises afterwards, "as if to be detected." The instinct of the pettiest criminal was to flee the scene of a crime, Phillips said, and had Courvoisier wished to get a six- or eight-hour head start on any pursuers "in these days of speedy progress," he could have done so very easily. Phillips was obviously thinking of the amazing new railway network, which could have sped the culprit to the other end of the country in no time. He didn't need to add that Courvoisier could also as easily have slipped away to the Steam Packet Wharf and made for the Continent, where his chances of capture would have been very slim indeed.

The fact that Courvoisier subsequently confessed to having done exactly what Phillips deemed incredible—committing the most terrible crime on a whim, staying in the house after its commission and making no attempt to flee—certainly deepens the puzzle. Mulling over the first reports of the case, Sir Robert Adair, Lord William's old family friend, made this astute remark about it: "the robbery part of this dreadful deed was so clumsy that I cannot think robbery was the motive. I fear it was diabolical revenge, for some trifle, a hasty word perhaps operating on a vindictive temper. For what else could have armed the villain's hand against such a good man?" Sir Robert's suggestion is more subtle than simply saying—as many people did—that Courvoisier might be mad (which few believed, because he looked like such a well-behaved and conventional young man). What Sir Robert imagines is a sudden, murderous antipathy, triggered by "some trifle"—something like "valet-rage." The killer might have found Lord William derisible, disgusting even, and viewed his death as little more than the dispatching of something useless (rather like the inference, in *Jack Sheppard*, that the murder of the ageing, unpleasant Mrs. Wood is not so very lamentable). That would make some sense of the casualness of the murder, and square with Courvoisier's claim to have developed a desire to escape and live a carefree "Jack Sheppard" life, funded by occasional thefts. Possibly he was used to supplementing his wages by constant petty thievery, and the only way he thought he could get away with a more substantial heist was by murdering the only witness and removing himself from suspicion by *not* running away.

But the sort of psychopath who might kill to punish a perceived slight (the slighter the better) would usually have a history of disturbing behaviour, or oddness, and the young valet was never complained of in this way; on the contrary he seemed consistently quiet and inoffensive, as Lady Julia Lockwood and many others testified. Why would he risk so much for so little?

"Cards and women, Watson: great motive-makers," says Sherlock Holmes, and one of the most glaring omissions from Phillips's list of motives—but understandable, given the mores of the time—is sex. The only hint of Courvoisier having romantic feelings towards anyone, in England or back home in Switzerland, is the reference to Henriet and Betzi in his letter to his sisters, but he is mostly concerned there in dismissing any serious interest. His special mention of the servant Catherine in his letter to the head servant at Kearsney Abbey also seems perfunctory, a social politeness. The very absence of talk of a sweetheart, or gossip about him and female servants (despite the press straining to find any details of his life in the weeks between the arrest and the execution), suggests that the 23-year-old was either fairly inactive sexually or very discreet; "I never heard a very little from him about the female servants," James Leech told the police under examination, while Courvoisier's uncle Louis said (to emphasize his nephew's rectitude), "I do not know of his having any female acquaintance." But what about male acquaintance? In 1840, the pursuit of same-sex attractions would have required considerable discretion, though service itself was a profession with plentiful sexual opportunities for employers and employees, and mutually supportive networks must have been in operation, then as ever.

Lord William's sex life is similarly obscure. It is impossible to say at this distance in time what sort of attention he had required from the attendants at the baths in Lausanne— or what gender those attendants were. His devotion to his late wife and doting friendships with younger women such as Lady Hardy and Lady Westmorland suggest a conventional heterosexual profile, but only suggest it, and we have no idea if there was any sexual element in his relationship with his valet. But the detail about the removed truss, given in evidence to the police on the day of the murder by doctors Elsgood and Nussey (and never repeated, either at the committal hearing or at the trial), strikes a disturbing note, opening up the possibility that some transgressive tampering with the corpse may have taken place. When describing the murder scene, Henry Elsgood said that the "deceased wore a truss, which was removed" and John Nussey said that "from the position the truss was found in, in my opinion he had had some slight struggle." "Slight struggle" also appears in the notes. Why would Lord William have removed this garment at all in the middle of the night and be found lying on it?

Given these uncertainties, Courvoisier's true motives become even less knowable than before. But what about the method of the crime?

Only six weeks elapsed between the murder and Courvoisier's conviction, during five of which he was the prime, virtually the only, suspect. Once he confessed, there was not, strictly speaking, any need to pursue further the question of *what* exactly he had done. But with the leisure to look back at the surviving evidence, what exactly *was* done still seems open to question.

It's a pity that Judge Tindall thought "nothing turned on" information about the state of the corpse; it curtailed a whole line of further speculation about how the murder was committed. Lord William was found dead on the morning of 6 May with his throat cut. He had been murdered, certainly, but how? Many things in the accepted story seem highly unsatisfactory and unlikely: the valet apparently took one of the carving knives from the dining room, rolled up one sleeve of his coat and shirt, approached Lord William asleep in bed and slit his throat in one movement, during which his Lordship didn't wake or cry out, but convulsively moved his right hand and caught the passing impact of the knife with it. Then the murderer used a little towel to wipe the knife and his hands and put the towel over the dead man's face. The utter cleanliness of the bed hangings, walls, curtains and carpet while the bed, mattress and straw under-mattress were "completely saturated with gore" has always been a source of mystery, not adequately accounted for by Elsgood's suggestion (widely taken up) that a pillow must have been used to staunch the forceful upward escape of blood when the throat was cut into, the killer somehow managing to both cover a neck and cut it at the same time. Courvoisier never either confirmed or contradicted talk of the pillow. He didn't seem to have any opinion on the subject at all.

The pillow theory becomes more viable if one imagines an

accomplice on the scene. What if Courvoisier and Henry Carr were planning a life on the road together in the "Jack Sheppard" style Courvoisier outlined in his second confession, living off housebreaking and reneging on bills, and conspired to rob and kill Lord William as a first step? What if Henry Carr had slipped into the house on Tuesday evening via the area steps and kitchen door, which Courvoisier left unlocked for him on his return from the pub? What if Carr stripped to kill Lord William, while Courvoisier juggled with the pillow? These scenarios seem possible, but still don't quite add up. The direction and forceful exit of the blood remains a stumbling block.

There is, however, another way in which the murderer, or murderers, could have effected the throat-cutting, which fits with the evidence. On his last night in Newgate, after the strip of cloth was found in his pocket, Courvoisier said he had planned to kill himself by bleeding to death. Whether or not this was another fantasy on the part of the condemned man, it shows he knew all about this way of killing and may have had experience of it (in the bleeding of animals, for instance, on his father's smallholding back home). Perhaps Lord William did not die from the throat wound, but was dead already when that cut was made. Perhaps Courvoisier did exactly what he told the turnkeys in Newgate he was thinking of doing to himself; applied a ligature or tourniquet and bled his victim to death first. Could it be that Lord William was overpowered in some way, even as early as when he went downstairs and caught Courvoisier stealing (if he did indeed do that), and was killed, as it were, in stages? The scene that Courvoisier describes of their angry interview in the drawing room has so much the ring of truth about it, but the idea that an employer would confront an errant servant in that way, resolve to sack him and then *go back to sleep* in an unlocked room stretches credulity entirely. If Lord William did come downstairs in the night in the way described by Courvoisier, I doubt he went back upstairs alive.

If Lord William was overpowered, or drugged, or strangled first (there was that scarf found round his neck by Dr. Elsgood) and killed that way or left to bleed, it would have been easy to make the single forceful chop to the neck later, there being no struggle on the part of the victim to overcome. Neither would there have been any risk of blood spurting out, since the pump was stopped. The blood would have all gone downwards, soaking the bed and mattress, and spilling on to the floor, as it did. The only precaution necessary to avoid getting stains on one's clothes in those circumstances would have been to roll back a sleeve and be dexterous.

No intruders would have murdered in that more complicated way, that much is obvious, but cutting the throat would be necessary to make the killing look as if it had been more "normal" and spontaneous, a sudden assault. And one last detail also fits with this theory: John Nussey at Bow Street said that the victim's right hand was raised towards the throat in what he took to have been "involuntary at the time death took place . . . a convulsive effort at the moment, and the same instrument which cut the throat might have cut the thumb." It seems even more likely that the thumb was damaged in the same single, forceful cut at the throat if the right hand was already in such a convulsive posture, if the victim was, in other words, already dead.

Jack Sheppard ends with the gallows, but not every part of this story does. Despite the severity of his crime, high treason,

Edward Oxford was found not guilty by reason of insanity and sentenced to be detained indefinitely, spending the next twenty-four years in the lunatic asylum, Bedlam, where he behaved like a model inmate, learned several languages and turned out to be an excellent chess player. In 1864 he was transferred to the new criminal asylum at Broadmoor, "apparently sane," and was discharged three years later on condition that he emigrate to one of the colonies and never return. Perhaps if François Benjamin Courvoisier had pretended to be more peculiar, more unstable or even more foreign than he seemed, he too might have evaded the drop. Edward Oxford left for a new life in Melbourne, Australia, in 1867, aged forty-five. Under the adopted name of John Freeman, he made a living there as a painter and decorator, married, had children and lived to a good old age.

Henry Carr also seems to have got away, or disappeared. He was never heard of again after the trial, and is impossible to identify on subsequent census or death records among the many people with his name. Perhaps he carried out the plan he outlined to a fellow drinker at one of the Park Street pubs on the evening of 5 May 1840. It didn't seem suspicious at the time, but after the murder round the corner, the landlord of the pub went to the police to report that one of his customers, "a woman of loose character," had told him of a conversation she'd had at the bar with an unemployed servant called Carr on the day before Lord William's death, when he'd bought her a drink and invited her to toast his health. He was expecting his fortunes to turn very shortly, he told her, and was about to leave this country for Australia.

Persons of Interest

SIR ROBERT ADAIR (1763–1855), diplomat and close friend of Lord William Russell (and of his nephew young Lord William). He was a privy counsellor from 1828 and British Ambassador in Berlin from 1835 to 1841.

JOHN ADOLPHUS (1768–1845), lawyer and historian, who had the leadership of the Old Bailey for many years. Distinguished himself in his conduct of the defence in 1820 of Arthur Thistlewood and the other Cato Street Conspirators (who had planned to assassinate the Cabinet and trigger a rebellion). Other famous cases included those of the "Radlett murderer," John Thurtell, and the "Edgware Road murderer," James Greenacre, in 1823 and 1837, respectively.

WILLIAM HARRISON AINSWORTH (1805–82), Manchester-born lawyer and author of thirty-nine novels, including *Rookwood* (1834), *Jack Sheppard* (1839), *The Tower of London* (1840), *Guy Fawkes* (1841), *Old St. Paul's* (1841) and *The Lancashire Witches* (1849). He was at the centre of London literary life for decades, first as a contributor to *Fraser's Magazine*, then as editor of *Bentley's* and *Ainsworth's*, and latterly as the owner of the *New Monthly*. His wide circle of friends and admirers included Charles Dickens, Richard Harris Barham, Hablot K. Browne, George Cruikshank, Daniel Maclise, John Macrone and William Makepeace Thackeray.

RICHARD HARRIS BARHAM (1788–1845), author, under the pseudonym Thomas Ingoldsby, of the popular *Ingoldsby Legends*, which first appeared in *Bentley's Miscellany* in 1837. Convivial, witty and generous-spirited, he was a founder member of the Garrick Club and also an active clergyman, the rector of a parish adjacent to St. Paul's.

ELIZABETH BARRETT (1806–61), poet and woman of letters, much admired for her powers of intellect and precocious talent (she published her first book at the age of twelve). From her teens she was plagued by ill health and in 1839 had temporarily moved from her father's house in Wimpole Street in London to lodgings on the seafront at Torquay to convalesce. She had not at this date met Robert Browning, with whom she was to elope in 1846.

LADY SARAH BAYLY, *NÉE* VILLIERS (1779–1852), one of Lady Charlotte Russell's younger sisters, the widow of Charles Nathaniel Bayly, who in 1840 was living in an apartment at Hampton Court Palace.

SIR GEORGE BEAUMONT (1799–1845), not the 7th Baronet of that name (a leading art patron whose bequest to the nation helped found the National Gallery) but his heir, who succeeded to the baronetcy in 1827.

INSPECTOR HENRY BERESFORD, one of Richard Mayne's trusted "Reserve Division" officers, the forerunners of the detective force that formed in 1842.

EDWARD GEORGE EARLE BULWER, later Ist Baron Lytton (1803–73), poet, soldier, man of letters and Member of Parliament, whose bestselling novels included *Pelham* (1828), *Paul Clifford* (1830), *The Last Days of Pompeii* (1834), *Rienzi* (1835) and *The Coming Race* (1871). Born into an aristocratic family, he made a fortune as a writer, but his life was blighted by the acrimonious aftermath of his marriage to Rosina Wheeler; their public attacks on each other's characters fed the gossip columns for years. Bulwer changed his name to Bulwer-Lytton in 1844 (creating confusion in indexes ever after) and was made a baronet in 1866.

HENRY BURNETT (1811–93), music teacher and singer, who married Charles Dickens's sister Fanny in 1837.

HENRY CARR, formerly a servant in John Minet Fector's household at Kearsney Abbey, where he and François Courvoisier first met. Unemployed since early 1840.

FRANÇOIS BENJAMIN COURVOISIER, a manservant, born in Mont-la-Ville, Switzerland, in August 1816.

LOUIS COURVOISIER, the uncle of François Benjamin Courvoisier, butler to Sir George Beaumont.

CHARLES DICKENS (1812–70), former law office clerk and then newspaper and parliamentary reporter who found rapid and lasting success as a writer after the publication of *Sketches by Boz* (1836) and *The Posthumous Papers of the Pickwick Club* (1837).

GEORGE DOUBLEDAY, Lord William's groom. He and William York shared a room in lodgings in North Row, next to Shenton's livery stables.

JOHN ELLIOTSON (1791–1868), doctor, whose controversial mesmerism displays in the 1830s forced his resignation from University College, London, which he had helped to found. He later became interested in phrenology and was Charles Dickens's friend and family doctor.

JAMES ELLIS, manservant to Lord William Russell until 1 April 1840, when he left to join the household of the Earl of Mansfield. He had previously worked for Lord William's son Mr. William Russell.

HENRY ELSGOOD, a physician who had a practice based in Park Street, Mayfair.

JOHN MINET FECTOR JR. (1812–68), the wealthy heir to a banking empire in Dover and MP for Maidstone. Owner of Kearsney Abbey in Kent, and much else. In 1844–5 he sold all his Dover properties and moved to a mansion in Hyde Park.

JOHN FORSTER (1812–76), son of a Newcastle butcher and a dairy farmer's daughter, who trained as a lawyer and entered London literary life as literary critic of the *Examiner*, aged twenty-one. He was a great friend of Bulwer at one time, but his devotion to Dickens came to eclipse all others and his biography of the novelist, completed four years after Dickens's death, is his best-remembered work. In all his years in the south of England, he never lost his Geordie accent.

MARY HANNELL, cook, in Lord William's employment since 1838 and formerly in service with Lord Southampton. Her family was from Woburn and she was about thirty-three years old at the time of the murder.

LADY ANNE HARDY, *NÉE* BERKELEY (1788–1877), the wife of Vice-Admiral Sir Thomas Masterman Hardy, Nelson's second-in-command at the Battle of Trafalgar. Beautiful, clever and sociable, she was an intimate friend of Lord Byron, who was her distant relative.

FRANCIS HOBLER (1796–1869), attorney for the prosecution in the Courvoisier case and author of several works on law, coins and Roman history. His family were Swiss Protestants and originated from the same canton as Courvoisier.

ELIZABETH VASSALL FOX, BARONESS HOLLAND (1771–1845), wife of the 3rd Baronet, and a famous political hostess to Whig grandees such as Lord Brougham, Lord Macaulay and Lord Grey and the wits Samuel Rogers and Sydney Smith. She was known for her acerbic tongue and domineering temperament.

MARY ANNE KEELEY (1805–99), a popular and versatile actor, singer and theatre manager, who often appeared on stage with her husband, the comedian Robert Keeley. She played Smike in an early adaptation of Charles Dickens's *Nicholas Nickleby*, but her most famous role was as Jack Sheppard in the Adelphi's 1839 musical play of William Harrison Ainsworth's novel.

EDWIN LANDSEER (1802–73), one of the most successful and popular artists of the day, specializing in portraits of horses, dogs and duchesses. A great friend of William Russell and of Charles Dickens, and a fixture at both Gore House and Holland House in the 1830s.

LADY JULIA LOCKWOOD, *NÉE* GORE (C.1800–91), friend and neighbour of Lord William Russell, born in Dublin, daughter of the 2nd Earl of Arran. While still underage, she eloped with a rake, Robert Manners Lockwood, who ran through her money with spectacular speed and mistreated her for years. Her divorce from him was granted in 1837.

DANIEL MACLISE (1806–70), Irish artist, famous for historical subjects and portraits of contemporary writers (many of which were commissioned by *Fraser's Magazine* in the 1830s). He was a friend of both William Harrison Ainsworth and Charles Dickens.

WILLIAM MACREADY (1793–1873), one of the greatest actors of the day, famous for his Shakespearean roles. His many literary friends included Charles Dickens (who dedicated *Nicholas Nickleby* to him), Robert Browning and Alfred Tennyson.

SARAH MANCER, Lord William Russell's housemaid, in his employment since 1838. She had previously worked at Mivart's Hotel in Mayfair (later Claridge's) and for a tailor called Mr. Don in Golden Square. She was thirty-two or thirty-three years old at the time of the murder.

RICHARD MAYNE (1796–1868), one of the two "kings of Scotland Yard" (the other was Lieutenant Colonel Charles Rowan), a pivotally influential police commissioner in the early days of the Metropolitan force. He was knighted in 1851.

RICHARD MONCKTON MILNES, LATER 1ST BARON HOUGHTON (1809–85), worldly, restless and insatiably social poet and politician, the Conservative MP for Pontefract from 1837 to 1863. Milnes was a thrill-seeker and connoisseur of flagellation, who had been up in a balloon, down in a diving bell and later in life proposed to Florence Nightingale.

JOHN NUSSEY, Mayfair doctor and a Master of the Society of Apothecaries. Born and brought up in Yorkshire, his youngest sibling, Ellen (twenty-three years his junior), was the best friend and confidante of an obscure and disgruntled governess, Charlotte Brontë, yet to become a novelist.

COUNT ALFRED D'ORSAY (1801–52), the Adonis of Gore House and dandy paragon of the day. His affair with Marguerite Power, the Countess of Blessington, was uninterrupted by his marriage to her stepdaughter Lady Harriet Gardiner in 1827.

INSPECTOR NICHOLAS PEARCE, the young and ambitious police officer who moved the Russell murder investigation along dramatically and whose conduct during the case won him promotion when the Detective Division of the Met was formed in 1842.

HENRI PETHOUD, Lady Julia Lockwood's Swiss butler.

CHARLES PHILLIPS (1787–1859), Irish barrister and flamboyant public speaker, who had come to notice in his youth defending the Irish patriot Daniel O'Connell and Catholic Emancipation. After the Courvoisier case, criticism of his characteristic style and manner intensified and he never fully regained his former reputation. His nickname (probably not uttered in his hearing) was "Counsellor O'Garnish."

ELEANOR EMMA PICKEN (c.1820–98), a young woman who got to know the Dickens family through their mutual friends the Smithsons and who spent a holiday in Broadstairs with them in 1840. She published a short memoir of her acquaintance with the novelist in the year after his death, and revised it in 1881. Her married name was Eleanor Emma Christian.

CHARLOTTE PIOLAINE, the English wife of a French hotel proprietor, who ran the Hotel de Dieppe in Leicester Place, Leicester Square.

EDGAR ALLAN POE (1809–49), American poet, critic and journalist who in 1840 was working for *Graham's Magazine* in Philadelphia. *Tales of the Grotesque and Arabesque* had been published in 1839; his 1841 story "The Murders at the Rue Morgue" would later be hailed as a pioneering piece of detective fiction. He had married his thirteen-year-old cousin, Virginia Clemm, in 1836.

MARGUERITE POWER, COUNTESS OF BLESSINGTON (1789–1849), a famous beauty and woman of letters, of humble origins but ambitious alliances, the Earl of Blessington being her third husband (in 1818). She was editor of the influential *Keepsake* annuals and *The Book of Beauty*, and a prolific writer of criticism and verse, whose salon at Gore House became the most outré and lively of all the literary coteries.

LADY CHARLOTTE RUSSELL, *NÉE* VILLIERS (c.1771–1808), eldest daughter of the 4th Earl of Jersey, who married Lord William Russell in July 1789. She was the mother of seven children, one of whom died in infancy.

FRANCIS RUSSELL (1788–1861), 7th Duke of Bedford, the son of the
6th Duke, nephew of Lord William and brother of Lord John
Russell. Succeeded to the dukedom in 1839.

GEORGIANA RUSSELL, DUCHESS OF BEDFORD (1781–1853), the
lively and beautiful second wife of the 6th Duke of Bedford,
and mother of ten children. She was a generous hostess for two
decades at Woburn Abbey and at the Doune near Aviemore and,
like her husband, was a keen patron of the arts. After the Duke
died in 1839, she refused her lover Edwin Landseer's offer of
marriage, much to the painter's disappointment, though they
continued their affair.

JOHN RUSSELL, 6TH DUKE OF BEDFORD (1766–1839), Lord William Russell's older brother, who succeeded to the dukedom in
1802 and died in 1839. A great patron of the arts, he spent very
large sums on paintings, sculptures and new buildings for Woburn Abbey, and left considerable debts.

LORD JOHN RUSSELL (1792–1878), third son of the 6th Duke of Bedford, and the rising star of Whig politics in the 1830s. He had
played a pivotal role in the presentation of the 1831 Reform Bill
that radically altered Parliament and by the time of his uncle's
death was Secretary of State for the Colonies. He went on to be
Prime Minister three times and to be created an earl.

LORD [GEORGE] WILLIAM RUSSELL (1790–1846), second son of the
6th Duke of Bedford, who took up a diplomatic career after
serving in the army and Parliament. Known as "young Lord
William" in the family.

LORD WILLIAM RUSSELL (1767–1840), youngest son of the Marquess of Tavistock (who died in a hunting accident just before
he was born) and younger brother of the 6th Duke of Bedford.
Entered Parliament in January 1789 as a member for the county
of Surrey, but only held a ministerial post for a few months during Charles Grey's brief "Ministry of all the Talents" in 1806. In
1808 he lost heavily in Surrey and was returned for the Russell
family seat of Tavistock instead, which he held until 1819, and
then again from 1826 to 1831. Married Lady Charlotte Villiers
in 1789, and had seven children with her.

WILLIAM RUSSELL (1800–84), youngest son of Lord William Russell. He was appointed as Attorney General of the Duchy of Lancaster in 1833 and Accountant-General of the Court of Chancery six years later.

INSPECTOR JOHN TEDMAN, the Metropolitan Police officer put in charge of 14 Norfolk Street after Lord William's murder.

WILLIAM MAKEPEACE THACKERAY (1811–63), born in India but separated from his family aged five and educated in England, ending up at Cambridge, where he met Richard Monckton Milnes and Alfred Tennyson. Having lost the fortune which his father left him, he struggled to earn a living from writing and illustration until the success of *Vanity Fair* in 1848.

WILLIAM YORK, Lord William's coachman since 1836, aged twenty-five in 1840.

Notes

Abbreviations

CD	Charles Dickens
FC	François Benjamin Courvoisier
JF	John Forster
LWR	Lord William Russell
QV	Queen Victoria
WHA	William Harrison Ainsworth
WMT	William Makepeace Thackeray
AR	*The Annual Register or a View of History, and Politics, 1840* (London, 1841)
Ellis	S. M. Ellis, *William Harrison Ainsworth and His Friends* (2 vols., London, 1911)
Hobler	Francis Hobler, "An Account of the Murder of the Lord William Russell on the Night of the 5th & 6th May 1840," a scrapbook of documents relating to the investigation of the murder of Lord William Russell and the subsequent trial of François Benjamin Courvoisier, compiled by Francis Hobler, Harvard Law School Library, MS 4487
Hollingsworth	Keith Hollingsworth, *The Newgate Novel, 1830–1847: Bulwer, Ainsworth, Dickens & Thackeray* (Detroit, 1963)
John	*Cult Criminals: The Newgate Novels 1830–47*, ed. Juliet John (6 vols.; London, 1998): vol. 1, Edward

Bulwer-Lytton, *Paul Clifford;* vol. 2, Edward Bulwer-Lytton, *Eugene Aram;* vol. 5, William Harrison Ainsworth, *Rookwood;* vol. 6, William Harrison Ainsworth, *Jack Sheppard*

Kitton   *Charles Dickens by Pen and Pencil*, ed. Frederic G. Kitton (London, 1889)

LGWR   *Letters to Lord G. William Russell from Various Writers 1817–1845* (3 vols., London, 1915)

OB Courvoisier   *The Proceedings of the Old Bailey, 1674–1913,* Trial of François Benjamin Courvoisier, 18–20 June 1840, ref 1629, www.oldbaileyonline.org

OB Oxford   *The Proceedings of the Old Bailey, 1674–1913,* Trial of Edward Oxford, 6 July 1840, ref 1877, www.oldbaileyonline.org

Picken (1871)   E. E. Christian [Eleanor Emma Picken], "Reminiscences of Charles Dickens from a Young Lady's Diary," *Englishwoman's Domestic Magazine* (June 1871), issue 78, pp. 336–44

Picken (1888)   E. E. Christian [Eleanor Emma Picken], "Recollections of Charles Dickens," *Temple Bar: With Which is Incorporated Bentley's Miscellany* (April 1888), pp. 481–506

Pilgrim   *The Pilgrim Edition of the Letters of Charles Dickens*, ed. Madeline House, Graham Storey, et al., (12 vols., Oxford, 1965–2002)

Poland   *Report of the Trial of Courvoisier for the Murder of Lord William Russell, June 1840,* ed. Sir Harry Poland (London, 1918)

QV Journals   *The Journals of Queen Victoria*, www.queenvictoriasjournals.org

The Times   *The Times* Digital Archive, 1785–2012

WMT Letters   *The Letters and Private Papers of William Makepeace Thackeray*, ed. Gordon N. Ray (4 vols., London 1946)

Volumes cited in short form can be found in the bibliography.

INTRODUCTION

3 *This is really too horrid!*: *QV Journals*, 6 May 1840.

4 *placid and benignant . . . Aged and respected*: *Metropolitan Magazine*, 1 June 1840, vol. 28, issue 110, p. 170, and *Sunday Times*, 10 May 1840.

4 *many families at the west-end*: *The Times*, 8 May 1840.

5 *all men in power*: report of Lord Brougham's speech at the opening of Parliament, 16 January 1840, *AR*, p. 5.

5 *unfortunate spirit of insubordination*: report of Queen Victoria's speech at the opening of Parliament, 16 January 1840, *AR*, p. 2.

5 *general want of settledness*: *Monthly Review*, December 1839.

1. A LAST WALK

7 *I feel too old*: LWR to Lord G. William Russell, 16 May 1837, *LGWR*, vol. 3, p. 217.

8 old *Lord William*: John, 6th Duke of Bedford to Lord G. William Russell, 26 March 1822, *LGWR*, vol. 2, p. 6.

9 *an inglorious life*: John, 6th Duke of Bedford to Lord G. William Russell, 3 December 1832, *LGWR*, vol. 3, p. 32.

9 *a little deranged*: *QV Journals*, 8 November 1838.

9 *rum old chap*: Poland, p. 35.

10 *I have for very many years found a very pleasant home*: LWR to Lord G. William Russell, 26 June 1837, *LGWR*, vol. 3, p. 221.

10 *abundantly full of vexation*: *LGWR*, vol. 2, p. 255.

11 *I have heard that he acted very well*: Gore, *Nelson's Hardy and His Wife*, p. 106.

11 *as odd and absent as ever*: ibid., p. 129.

11 *jumping and hopping about*: ibid., p. 68.

11 *You swallowed it in one of your absent fits*: ibid., pp. 75–6.

12 *strange mode of life*: Blakiston, *Lord William Russell and His Wife*, p. 197.

12 *an unhappy wandering spirit*: ibid., pp. 64–5.

12 *had a great connection and friendship*: *QV Journals*, 8 November 1838.

12 quoiqu'il me parait un zero: Elizabeth Wynne, diary entry for 1 May 1807, Fremantle (ed.), *The Wynne Diaries*, vol. 3, p. 311.

14 *stupid old Swiss:* LWR to Lord G. William Russell, 10 June 1831, *LGWR,* vol. 2, p. 332.

14 *absolutely useless—of more plague than profit:* ibid.

15 *the confidants and agents:* quoted in Burnett, *Useful Toil,* p. 148.

17 *I left him in good health:* C. Barry, letter to *The Times,* 12 May 1840.

17 *close of itself: OB Courvoisier,* Sarah Mancer's evidence.

2. THE CRIME

20 *Oh no, I cannot; no, I cannot: The Times,* 11 May 1840.

21 *a great quantity of blood in the bed: OB Courvoisier,* John Tedman's evidence.

21 *some sharp instrument:* Henry Elsgood at the inquest, *The Times,* 7 May 1840.

22 *very deaf . . . from the position: The Times,* 7 May 1840.

22 *dark handkerchief:* "There was a dark handkerchief in the bed under his Lordship, and I noticed a great deal of blood in the bed," Daniel Young's testimony at the Bow Street committal hearing, as reported in *The Times,* 23 May 1840.

23 *It was very horrifying: The Times,* 7 May 1840.

23 *even a cat's foot:* Poland, p. 11.

24 *No thief would ever leave this property:* ibid., p. 45.

25 *but there were no traces of persons:* Lord Melbourne to QV, 6 May 1840, Benson and Esher (eds.), *The Letters of Queen Victoria,* vol. 1, pp. 278–9.

25 *I did not see the slightest marks of blood: The Times,* 7 May 1840.

26 *Some of you in the house . . . I examined everything: OB Courvoisier,* John Tedman's evidence.

27 *My God, someone has been robbing us!:* Poland, p. 28.

28 *the impression had been: QV Journals,* 7 May 1840.

29 *[He] is not in reduced circumstances:* FC at the inquest, *The Times*, 7 May 1840.

29 *a state of vigilance:* Poland, p. 13.

30 *the greater part of the night: The Times*, 7 May 1840.

30 *For a considerable number of years: The Times*, 10 May 1840.

30 *for the purpose of making enquiries*: "Dying Speeches & Bloody Murders: Crime Broadsides Collected by the Harvard Law School Library: Murder of Lord William Russell," seq. 188, http://broadsides.law.harvard.edu.

31 *the* bruit *which is made about this poor old man's death:* Toynbee (ed.), *Diaries of William Charles Macready*, 9 May 1840.

31 *Never glazed better:* Pope (ed.), *Diary of Benjamin Robert Haydon*, 6 May 1840.

31 *Here is a man shouting out:* WMT to Mrs. Carmichael-Smyth, May 1840, *WMT Letters*, vol. 1, p. 443.

31 *scientific persons:* Poland, p. 11.

32 *even that short interval: The Times*, 8 May 1840.

32 *by which means the fatal wound . . . a fear that they might implicate: The Times*, 7 May 1840.

34 *a Spaniard of dwarf stature*: *Examiner*, 3 November 1839.

35 *Beresford also tested Louisa Anstruther's evidence:* Hobler, seq. 192.

35 *I shall tell [Lord William] I understood him to say . . . and ought to pay for his forgetfulness:* Bridges, *Two Studies*, p. 19.

36 *He said he wished he had not come:* Poland, p. 25.

37 *closely questioned: The Times*, 8 May 1840.

37 *not perfectly satisfactory:* "Trial and Conviction of Courvoisier for the Murder of Lord W. Russell," *AR*, p. 244

37 *the new consort, Prince Albert, was sending frequent messages:* as reported in the *Morning Chronicle*, 9 May 1840.

37 *almost unprecedented: The Times*, 8 May 1840.

37 *which has excited a prodigious interest:* Pearce (ed.), *The Diaries of Charles Greville*, p. 188.

38 *to murder old John:* WMT to Mrs. Carmichael-Smyth, May 1840, *WMT Letters*, vol. 1, p. 443.

38 *remorseless hands have torn*: Mrs. Abdy, "Lines on the Death of Lord William Russell: written after passing his residence on Norfolk Street, on Saturday, May 9th," *Metropolitan Magazine*, 1 June 1840, vol. 28, issue 110, p. 170.

39 *the same, he said: Spectator*, 10 May 1840.

40 *done "little or nothing"*: Hobler, seq. 101.

41 *I suspected what he might say . . .* can you now look me in the face?: *OB Courvoisier*, Nicholas Pearce's evidence.

41 *When I find that the truth has been spoken: Caledonian Mercury*, 25 June 1840.

42 *a middle-sized man, rather stoutly made: The Times*, 12 May 1840.

3. "THIS NIGHTMARE OF A BOOK"

45 *without a particle of conceit:* Ellis, vol. 1, p. 262.

45 *You see what a pretty fellow:* ibid., p. 260.

47 *low smoking rooms, the common barbers' shops: Examiner*, 3 November 1839.

48 *chances of illuminating mankind:* John, vol. 2, chapter 7.

48 *We say, let your rogues in novels act like rogues:* [WMT], "Horae Catnachianae."

48 *the jolly, bold and free:* from a song in *Paul Clifford* called "The Love of Our Profession; or, The Robber's Life" (John, vol. 1, p. 134), which ends:

> Oh! there never was life like the Robber's—so
>   Jolly, and bold, and free;
> And its end—why, a cheer from the crowd below,
>   And a leap from a leafless tree!

49 *a* purely flash *song:* WHA, preface to *Rookwood* (1834).

49 *Are you quite* sure: Ellis, vol. 1, p. 253.

49 *It is doing famously well here:* WHA to James Crossley, 6 May 1834, Ellis, vol.1, p. 257.

50 *eagerly examined and discussed:* ibid., p. 258.

50 *Was he not the double of d'Orsay?*: ibid., p. 266.

51 *a swallow-tail coat with a very high velvet collar:* Kitton, p. 19.

51 *including those worn by the redoubtable Jack Sheppard:* CD, "A Visit to Newgate," *Sketches by Boz* (1836).

52 *after the ride [Mr. Ainsworth] has given us:* ibid.

53 *excessively interesting:* quoted in Collins, *Dickens and Crime*, p. 259.

53 *young Lord William Russell recommended it:* in a letter to his wife, n.d., 1839, Blakiston, *Lord William Russell and His Wife*, p. 420. *Nicholas Nickleby* reminded him forcibly of his own schooldays: "Dickens (the author) is the modern Fielding & quite equal to him in many descriptions. Read also *Oliver Twist*."

53 *some of Dickens's nonsense: Pilgrim*, vol. 1, p. 417, n. 1.

53 *a more ferocious and ghastly deed:* Horne, *A New Spirit of the Age*, vol. 1, p. 19.

53 *to illustrate ancient and modern London:* Ellis, vol. 1, pp. 332–3.

53 *The truth is, to write for the mob:* ibid., pp. 336–7.

55 *Ay, ay, it's all bob, my covey!:* John, vol. 6, p. 17.

56 *those Froissarts and Holinsheds of crime:* ibid., p. 86.

56 *if my name should become as famous as theirs:* ibid., p. 55.

57 *treading upon the point of their toes:* ibid., p. 180.

57 *"Leave go!" thundered Blueskin:* ibid., p. 181.

58 *according to his biographer, S. M. Ellis:* Ellis, vol. 1, p. 351.

59 *Bentley's "fetters":* ibid., p. 387n.

60 *I trust [it] will be as* popular: ibid., p. 344.

60 *should not be lost sight of in the* advertisement: Bleakley, *Jack Sheppard*, p. 88.

60 *without having occasion to refer to:* Barham, *Life and Letters*, vol. 2, p. 91.

61 *a hydra-headed, extra-literary phenomenon:* "at least the equal of anything in popular entertainment in the present [twentieth] century," according to the critic Keith Hollingsworth in *The Newgate Novel*, p. 140.

61 *a serial by "M. H. Ainsforth":* in the *Sunday Times*, April 1841.

62 *Being under the dominion of Satan: The Times*, 8 July 1840.

62 Jack Sheppard *is a bad book:* Hollingsworth, p. 142.

62 *pernicious . . . poisonous: Examiner,* 3 November 1839.

63 [*The author of* Jack Sheppard] *puts us out of all patience:* Edgar Allan Poe in *Graham's Magazine,* quoted in Thompson, *Fierce Fiction,* p. 110.

63 *little Jack Sheppard's christening dinner: Pilgrim,* vol.1, p. 474, n. 3.

63 *We notice this "romance" with very great reluctance:* JF review of *Jack Sheppard, Examiner,* 3 November 1839.

64 *absurd and unreal:* [WMT], "Horae Catnachianae," p. 407.

64 *We are sick of heroic griefs, passions, tragedies:* ibid., p. 408.

64 *a wholesome nausea:* WMT, *Catherine,* p. 132.

65 *no literary merit whatever:* see the later Victorian edition of *Catherine* used on Project Gutenberg, www.gutenberg.org.

65 *and so Jack Sheppard makes his appearance:* WMT, *Catherine,* pp. 132–3.

66 *the whole London public:* ibid., p. 132.

66 *Come, all ye jolly covies:* "The Faker's New Toast," Hanchant (ed.), *The Newgate Garland.*

67 *All my larnin' . . . The Surrey, and the Cobug: New Monthly Magazine* (January 1840), p. 119.

68 *gross and violent excitements: Monthly Review,* December 1839.

68 *those changes and intensities that mark our social condition and divisions: Monthly Review,* December 1839.

69 *Sins of coarseness and affectation and latitudinarianism:* Elizabeth Barrett to Mary Russell Mitford, 6 March 1840, Hudson et al. (eds.), *The Brownings' Correspondence,* vol. 4, p. 249.

69 *I have been struck by the great danger in these times:* Mary Russell Mitford to Elizabeth Barrett, 3[0] January 1840, ibid., p. 232.

4. THE PLAY

71 *"Jack Sheppard"—have you been to see "Jack Sheppard"?: Monthly Review,* December 1839.

71 *Jack Sheppard is the attraction at the* Adelphi: *Examiner,* 3 November 1839.

72 *ASTONISHING AND ELECTRICAL Representation:* advertisement in the *Examiner,* 3 November 1839.

73 *I thought [Jack] was in Newgate:* Buckstone, *Jack Sheppard,* act 3, scene 4.

73 *when I slipped them off it was no stage slip:* Goodman, *The Keeleys,* p. 62.

73 *One young fan:* ibid., p. 211.

74 *The fate of the Thief-taker and the Thief:* Penny Satirist, 2 November 1839.

74 *the scenic effects are really most surprisingly good:* JF in the *Examiner,* 3 November 1839.

75 *depravity, however covered by bravado:* Bleakley, *Jack Sheppard,* p. 92.

75 *Henry Neville, the future actor, recalled later:* Ellis, vol. 1, p. 365n.

75 *I became so familiar with the fascinating drama:* Goodman, *The Keeleys,* p. 11.

75 *charming little figure:* Ellis, vol. 1, p. 365, n. 1.

76 *what are considered well educated and superior classes:* Monthly Review, December 1839.

76 *which catches the manners as they rise:* Horne, *A New Spirit of the Age,* vol. 2, pp. 91–2.

77 *In a box of the stone jug I was born:* G. H. Rodwell, "Nix My Dolly, Pals, Fake Away," music from *The Romance of Jack Sheppard* (1839).

78 *as popular in the drawing-rooms of St. James's:* Ellis, vol. 1, p. 252.

78 *whistled by every dirty guttersnipe:* ibid., p. 366.

79 *Corelli or Viotti:* Barham, *Life and Letters,* vol. 2, pp. 107–8.

79 Nix My Dolly . . . *travelled everywhere:* Ellis, vol. 1, p. 366.

79 *recollected by a young friend:* Eleanor Emma Picken (later E. E. Christian) wrote two versions of her memories of this summer, "Reminiscences of Charles Dickens from a Young Lady's Diary," in *Englishwoman's Domestic Magazine,* June

1871, and "Recollections of Charles Dickens" eighteen years later in *Temple Bar.*

80 *Go where you will by night or day:* Picken doesn't specify this text, but it is the likely one: "Here's a Health to the Queen of England or, Britain's Hopes," National Library of Scotland, shelfmark Crawford. EB. 1658.

80 *and a good many of the others:* Picken (1871), p. 341.

81 *Public morality and public decency:* JF in the *Examiner,* 3 November 1839.

81 *There is no doubt:* John Hamilton Reynolds in *Fraser's Magazine,* February 1840.

82 *At the Cobourg:* WMT to his mother, 1–2 December 1839, *WMT Letters,* vol. 1, p. 395.

82 *"A Young Jack Sheppard" . . . "Juvenile Jack Sheppards" . . . two other ten-year-old "Jack Sheppards" . . . A sparky nine-year-old:* cases reported in the *Examiner,* 3 November 1839, 8 December 1839 and 29 November 1839.

83 *Jack was not felt to be an enemy of society:* Hollingsworth, p. 141.

83 *Again Jack Sheppard!!!:* *Examiner,* 1 December 1839.

83 *A youth called Murphy . . . An eighteen-year-old who had robbed a house in Woolwich . . . Three youths in the Preston House of Correction:* cases reported in the *Examiner,* 6 September 1840 and 17 November 1839, and *Chambers's Edinburgh Journal,* December 1841.

84 *I say, wasn't it well acted?:* "The March of Knowledge," *Penny Satirist,* 14 December 1839.

5. THE INVESTIGATION

87 *appeared much to regret the premature and lamentable death:* *The Times,* 13 May 1840.

88 *[though] we have hardly been able . . . to think of anything else:* Francis, 7th Duke of Bedford, to Lord G. William Russell, 22 May 1840, *LGWR,* vol. 3, p. 301.

88 *wrote to Lord William of his fears:* Sir Robert Adair to Lord G. William Russell, *LGWR,* vol. 3, pp. 303–4.

89 *Considering the modes of proceeding: Examiner*, 17 May 1840.

89 *really pulled to pieces:* Hobler, seq. 184.

90 *to the place where the linen was: OB Courvoisier*, John Tedman's evidence.

90 *I was busy searching another part of the room: OB Courvoisier*, George Collier's evidence.

90 *The Courvoisier Infatuation: Examiner*, 28 June 1840.

91 *He is rather ill-looking:* Pearce (ed.), *The Diaries of Charles Greville*, p. 189.

92 *The circumstances of the case are certainly most extraordinary:* ibid., p. 188.

92 *a few pounds at different times:* Hobler, seq. 145.

93 *one historian of Dover:* Sencicle, *Banking on Dover*.

94 *did great credit to his ingenuity and neatness of hand:* Elliotson, *Illustrations of Phrenology*, p. 16.

95 *Dear Sir, You will think it perhaps a long time:* FC to an unknown correspondent, 28 April 1840, published in *Southern Star and London and Brighton Patriot*, 5 July 1840.

96 *Chére Claris:* FC to his sisters Claris and Clémence, 13 April 1840, ibid. The full text of the letter is as follows (complete with numerous spelling mistakes):

Londre, le 13 Avril, 1840
Chére Claris,
    Je suis presque obblige de te manqué de parole, car jai beaucoup a faire apresent. Je pance que ma soeur sait que jai change de place. Jai quitte M. Fector comme tu le pansoit, mais pas pour me rentouere en suisse, mais poar arlez avec un vieux de 74 an, je nai pas beacoup a faire seulement, que nous avons beaucoup de visite cette semaine, et tu soit que quand il fauit servi de valet de chambre a 3 Monsieur et famme de chambre pour 2 dames quil toujour assez a faire, mais après cette semaine je n'naurai pluss que mon bon vieux, sest vrai quil est comme sont presque tout les vieux, (je vous dire trés embletant) ma Chère Clèmence tu croi que jétoit faché en

lisant tes petits conseils bien le contrere. Je t'en remercie,
et je te dirai que si je me marie en Angleterre que se ne
cera pas avec Henriet, malgré quelle soit bonne fille. Je soit
bien que l'argent ne rend pas l'homme heureux, mais de
ce mariez et se voir dans misère, ne le rende pas heureux
non plus, tu me disent de te faire le d'etail de ce que sont
devenue. Hte et Betzi, Betzi a quitte sa place et elle est
allér premiere fille de maison dans la mème famille ou sa
taute est femme de charge.

99 *I am by some jolter-headed enemies:* CD to R. H. Horne [?February 1840], *Pilgrim*, vol. 2, pp. 20–21.

99 *Dickens was at luncheon at his house:* Picken (1888), p. 499.

100 *frequently just at the time . . . he is full of terror & horror:* Ilchester (ed.), *Letters of . . . Lady Holland*, pp. 184–5.

100 *But could it be true, as she asked Miss Mitford:* Elizabeth Barrett to Mary Russell Mitford, 11 January 1842, Miller (ed.), *Elizabeth Barrett to Miss Mitford*, p. 99.

101 *It was I, it was me that did it:* account of the trial of Edward Oxford, *Examiner*, 12 July 1840.

101 *a vast number of the nobility and gentry: AR,* Chronicle for June 1840.

101 *It was indeed a most awful and providential escape: QV Journal,* 11 June 1840.

102 *John Tedman . . . had noticed this habit quite independently: OB Oxford,* John Tedman's evidence.

102 *how the stoutest man stood appalled:* Poland, p. 80.

103 *the excitement he had caused in the public mind: The Times,* 8 July 1840.

103 *It's a great pity they couldn't suffocate that boy:* CD to JF, ?12 June 1840, *Pilgrim*, vol. 1, pp. 81–2.

103 *brimful of conceit:* CD to the *Daily News*, 9 March 1846.

104 *Oh, why didn't he rob some rich old gentleman:* CD, *Oliver Twist*, chapter XLIII.

105 *of unsound mind . . . very much—generally sea-voyages:* account

of the trial of Edward Oxford, *Examiner*, 12 July 1840, and *OB Oxford*, Susannah Phelps's evidence.

105 *most earnest . . . declaration of innocence:* The Times, 8 June 1840.

105 *no appearance of disturbed sleep:* ibid.

106 *A rumour went round:* The Times, 15 June 1840.

106 *of frequenting houses of bad repute:* ibid.

107 *a teaspoon and salt spoon: OB Courvoisier*, John Tedman's evidence.

107 *if not A Principal:* Hobler, seq. 192.

109 *supposed to have belonged . . . completely saturated with blood:* The Times, 18 June 1840.

109 *the fair portion of his auditory:* Grant, *Portraits of Public Characters*, p. 186.

110 *I have not the slightest doubt:* Henderson, *Recollections*, pp. 203–8.

110 *grave suspicion:* Lord Russell of Liverpool, *Though the Heavens Fall*, p. 45.

6. THE TRIAL

111 *dressed up to the eyes:* Ballantine, *Some Experiences of a Barrister's Life*, vol. 1, p. 89.

112 *a great interest:* Poland, p. 2.

112 *excited and perspiring:* Ballantine, *Some Experiences of a Barrister's Life*, vol. 1, p. 89.

112 *the house was therefore shown to be left:* Poland, p. 7.

112 *anything found in the box on any occasion:* ibid., p. 14.

113 *how it was that a good man became a criminal:* ibid., p. 6.

113 *Sarah Mancer . . . had demanded an interview with Phillips:* Freeman's Journal, 30 June 1840.

113 *Now, attend to me, on the oath you have taken: OB Courvoisier*, cross-examination of Sarah Mancer.

116 *I was very much alarmed and agitated: OB Courvoisier*, Mary Hannell's evidence.

116 *If he moved a chair or anything:* ibid.

117 *the shirt-collar was wide open:* OB Courvoisier, Henry Els-
     good's evidence.

117 *tucked in within the sheets:* John Tedman's evidence at Bow
     Street committal hearing, as reported in *The Times*, 23 May
     1840.

117 *might have been held directly over the mouth of the vessel:* OB
     Courvoisier, Henry Elsgood's evidence.

117 *see entirely into the wound:* OB Courvoisier, John Nussey's
     evidence.

118 *[the victim] looked as if he were asleep:* OB Courvoisier, John
     Tedman's evidence.

118 *a few minutes:* OB Courvoisier, John Baldwin's evidence.

119 *one or two ... I will not swear I have not spoken to twenty:*
     ibid.

120 *with a gentleman:* OB Courvoisier, Charlotte Piolaine's evi-
     dence.

121 *tossed and gored:* Atlay, *Famous Trials*, p. 610.

122 *much agitated:* Ballantine, *Some Experiences of a Barrister's
     Life*, vol. 1, p. 89.

123 *I do not think I took all the articles quite out:* OB Courvoisier,
     Henry Beresford's evidence.

123 *marks of any thing bloody [. . .] I should consider a torn shirt-
     front:* OB Courvoisier, George Collier's evidence.

124 *Very likely I may—I do expect it:* OB Courvoisier, Nicholas
     Pearce's evidence.

125 *What did you mean by saying you* think *you could swear it?:*
     OB Courvoisier, cross-examination of Charlotte Piolaine.

126 *Do you, like other women, converse with your husband:* ibid.

126 *I am an acquaintance of the prisoner's:* OB Courvoisier, Henry
     Carr's evidence.

127 *Tell Mr. Phillips I consider my life is in his hands:* Atlay,
     Famous Trials, p. 9.

127 *and the most intense anxiety was manifested:* The Times,
     22 June 1840.

128 *his case had not been left to the ordinary instruments of justice:*
     Poland, p. 74.

128 *Ambition's vision, glory's bauble: The Times,* 22 June 1840.

130 *most crowded court ever witnessed: Hull Packet,* 26 June 1840.

130 *even simplicity of character: Newcastle Courant,* 26 June 1840.

130 *The prisoner at the bar was in my service:* ibid.

131 *We find him* guilty . . . *François Benjamin Courvoisier, you have been found guilty: The Times,* 22 June 1840.

132 *wicked . . . wholly inexcusable:* CD to the editor of the *Morning Chronicle* [?21 June 1840], *Pilgrim,* vol. 2, pp. 86–7.

132 "*very much*" *wanted to have published:* CD to John Black, 21 June 1840, *Pilgrim,* vol. 2, p. 86.

132 *At the risk of giving some offence:* CD to the editor of the *Morning Chronicle* [?21 June 1840], *Pilgrim,* vol. 2, pp. 86–7.

134 *but in my opinion he was absolutely bound to do so:* "A Templar" to the editor of the *Morning Chronicle,* 23 June 1840, *Pilgrim,* vol. 2, p. 492.

134 *I recognize the right of any counsel:* CD to the editor of the *Morning Chronicle,* 26 June 1840, *Pilgrim,* vol. 2, p. 91.

7. IN THE STONE JUG

135 *impossible to describe: Hull Packet,* 26 June 1840.

135 *a huge black pen:* CD, "A Visit to Newgate," *Sketches by Boz* (1836).

136 *a clumsy attempt to kill himself:* reported in the *Morning Chronicle,* 7 July 1840.

137 *As I told you on Friday:* British Library, add 28721/I :184, f 27–8, letter from Thomas France to Christopher Hodson Esq., 25 June 1840 (containing a transcript of FC's first confession).

138 *He told me, rather crossly:* this and following remarks by FC are from "Confession of Courvoisier," Poland, pp. 112–13.

139 *and some more I took after the cook went to bed:* ibid., p. 115.

140 *but had not the least idea of taking it:* ibid., p. 114.

141 *as if I told the truth I should not be believed:* ibid.

142 *A valet to Lord William Russell:* anon., "Verses on F. B. Courvoisier Now Lying under Sentence of Death for the Murder of his Master, Lord William Russell," Bodleian Library, Broadside Ballads Online, Johnson Ballads, 644.

143 *some more letters addressed to the assassin:* "Original Letters of Courvoisier, the Assassin of Lord William Russell," *Southern Star and London and Brighton Patriot*, 5 July 1840.

144 *I took a towel which was on the back of a chair:* Poland, p. 113.

145 *he had no clothes on:* Henderson, *Recollections*, p. 155.

145 *turned up my coat and shirt sleeve:* Poland, p. x.

145 *Nothing at all of the kind had occurred:* "Confession of Courvoisier to Sheriff Evans," *Morning Chronicle*, 25 June 1840.

146 *I went to the side of the bed:* ibid.

146 *When he drew the knife across the throat:* ibid.

147 *He declared, and he wished the Sheriff to let it be known:* *Examiner*, 28 June 1840.

147 *first step on the downward path: The Times*, 26 June 1840.

148 *[Courvoisier] ascribes his crimes: Examiner*, 28 June 1840.

149 *Sir,—A statement to the effect:* WHA to the editor of *The Times*, 7 July 1840.

150 *Sir—I observe in your journal:* William Evans to the editor of *The Times*, 8 July 1840.

150 *impugning my statement . . . I beg to say:* WHA to the editor of the *Morning Chronicle*, 11 July 1840.

151 *if the statement of Mr. Ainsworth had remained uncontradicted: Examiner*, 12 July 1840.

152 *false statements . . . If there are any contradictions: Era*, 12 July 1840.

153 *in a paper under the thumb of my hand:* FC's third confession (4 July), *Morning Chronicle*, 8 July 1840.

154 *he feared he was a thief: Examiner*, 28 June 1840.

154 *acted unjustly: The Times*, 8 July 1840.

154 *a young woman and two youths: London Evening Standard*, 24 June 1840.

155 *it was not worth the while to speak of it:* FC's third confession (4 July), *Morning Chronicle*, 8 July 1840.

155 *he cannot have told the truth:* Sir Robert Adair to Lord G. William Russell, 30 June 1840, *LGWR*, vol. 3, p. 307.

156 *Oh! when I think how much evil I have done: Era*, 12 July 1840.

156 *Look at the documents which came from the prison:* WMT, "Going to See a Man Hanged."

157 *anxious to see the effect on the public mind:* Richard Monckton Milnes (disguised as "X") in WMT, "Going to See a Man Hanged."

157 *No politics, [and] as much fun and satire as I can muster:* WMT to Alexander Blackwood, 29 June 1840, *WMT Letters,* vol. 1, pp. 450–51.

158 *The town was full of it:* Goodman, *The Keeleys,* p. 61.

158 *[The murderer] says that the first idea of crime:* ibid., pp. 61–2.

8. THE EXECUTION

159 *You had almost reached the very verge:* Newcastle Courant, 10 July 1840.

160 *but the evasions, subterfuges, and inconsistencies: Era,* 12 July 1840.

160 *He seemed to pay attention: Bristol Mercury,* 11 July 1840.

161 *in the removal it might have been lost:* ibid.

161 *thirty years later recorded what was said:* in Picken (1888).

164 *what is being done . . . the people wedged him in so tightly:* Kitton, pp. 142–3.

166 *You must not think me inhospitable in refusing to sit up:* WMT to Richard Monckton Milnes, 5 July 1840, *WMT Letters,* vol. 1, p. 451.

166 *The light coming through the cell-window:* WMT, "Going to See a Man Hanged."

167 *It is curious that a murder is a great inspirer of jokes:* ibid.

168 *aristocratic brutes: Hampshire Independent,* 11 July 1840.

169 *evincing the fearful interest: Era,* 12 July 1840.

170 *a "horrible fascination" about the punishment of death:* CD to the *Daily News,* 28 February 1846.

170 *The actor Charles Kean:* Elliotson, *Illustrations of Phrenology,* p. 15.

171 *the greatest confusion:* ibid.

171 *great murmur . . . more awful, bizarre, and indescribable:* WMT, "Going to See a Man Hanged."

172 *I am not ashamed to say that I shut my eyes:* ibid.

172 *The moment the rope was suspended:* Inverness Courier, 15 July 1840.

172 *But another paper contradicted this flatly:* Bristol Mercury, 11 July 1840.

173 *All was brightness and promise:* CD, Barnaby Rudge (1841), chapter 77.

174 *From the moment of my arrival:* CD to the Daily News, 28 February 1846.

175 *I fully confess that I came away:* WMT, "Going to See a Man Hanged."

175 *A ghastly night in Hades:* Kitton, p. 143.

175 *It was so loathsome, pitiful and vile a sight:* CD to the Daily News, 28 February 1846.

176 *I was brought up by honest Parents:* anon., "The Lament of François Courvoisier," in "The Execution of Francis [*sic*] Courvoisier for the Murder of Lord William Russell, opposite the Debtor's Door, This Day" (London, 1840).

177 *Even at three o'clock in the afternoon:* anon., "Courvoisier: A Sketch Taken in Newgate," Odd Fellow, 25 July 1840.

9. THE AFTERMATH

178 *the blue devils . . . I can't do my work:* WMT to Mrs. Carmichael-Smyth, 6?–18 July 1840, WMT Letters, vol. 1, p. 453.

178 *the magazine 'We':* WMT, "Going to See a Man Hanged."

180 *F.B. Courvoisier, Taken from Life:* Tussaud exhibition catalogue, 1840.

180 *Cruder waxwork figures:* "Summary Vengeance," unattributed newspaper cutting, Hobler, seq. 412.

181 *it was a large and "powerful" specimen:* Elliotson, Illustrations of Phrenology, p. 17.

182 *distribution of the £400 reward money:* unattributed newspaper cutting, n.d., "Dying Speeches & Bloody Murders: Crime Broadsides Collected by the Harvard Law School Library:

Murder of Lord William Russell," seq. 214, http://broadsides .law.harvard.edu.

183 *Whether [Phillips's behaviour] accords or not: Examiner,* 28 June 1840.

183 *How much worse was Mr. Phillips's attempt: Examiner,* 3 November 1849.

184 *SARAH MANCER, the housemaid:* quoted in *Littell's Living Age,* 26 January 1850.

184 *Francis Hobler wrote bitterly of the Russell family's later negligence:* Hobler, seq. 412.

185 *A man of the world by profession:* Henry Adams, *The Education of Henry Adams* (1907), chapter 8.

185 *I am solemnly convinced:* CD to the editor of *The Times,* 13 November 1849, *Pilgrim,* vol. 5, p. 645.

186 *his sayings and doings being served up in print:* CD to the editor of *The Times,* 17 November 1849, *Pilgrim,* vol. 5, p. 653.

186 *the wise and great relaxation of our criminal code:* "A Day with Lord Lytton," Jerrold (ed.), *The Best of All Good Company,* pp. 184–5.

187 *show [criminals] as they really are:* CD, 1841 preface to *Oliver Twist.*

187 *familiarize the imagination with deeds of blood: Examiner,* 12 July 1840.

187 *and on their physical, intellectual, and moral character:* reported in the *Penny Satirist,* 23 March 1843.

188 *the deification of great thieves:* "Felon Literature," *Chambers's Edinburgh Journal,* December 1841.

188 *I regret much, my dear W.H.A.:* Ellis, vol. 1, p. 377.

188 *having been given to understand:* quoted in Bleakley, *Jack Sheppard,* p. 87.

189 *Good heavens! Is he still alive?:* Ellis, vol. 2, p. 264.

189 *I did intend to introduce the republication:* Ellis, vol. 1, pp. 378–9.

190 *Intensely amusing as it is:* Hibbard (ed.), *The Book of Poe,* p. 114.

192 *My ordinary pulse is 72:* CD to W. H. Wills, 23 January 1870,
　　　Pilgrim, vol. 12, p. 470.
193 *the children's governess had apparently run mad:* reported in
　　　The Times, 9 June 1840.
193 *It is not generally known:* Robert Blake Overton to Lord John
　　　Russell, 16 May 1840, Hobler, seq. 479–81.
194 *I never had the remotest intention:* Ellis, vol. 1, p. 378.
195 *moral curiosity:* Collins, *Dickens and Crime,* p. 260.
195 *I plead guilty to the charge of Jacobitism:* anon., "Mr. W. Har-
　　　rison Ainsworth at Little Rockley," in Yates (ed.), *Celebrities at
　　　Home.*
195 Jack Sheppard *did its evil work of popularity:* Horne, *A New
　　　Spirit of the Age,* vol. 1, pp. 12–13.

POSTSCRIPT: UNANSWERED QUESTIONS

197 *I began two or three times not to like the place:* Poland, p. 112.
198 *When I find that the truth has been spoken: Caledonian Mer-
　　　cury,* 25 June 1840.
198 *with a wild imploring look:* WMT, "Going to See a Man
　　　Hanged."
199 *Une récompense a été annoncée: Gazette des Tribunaux,* 10
　　　May 1840.
200 *it seems pretty clear that no credit can be given: The Times,*
　　　27 June 1840.
200 *against a venerable and noble master: The Times,* 8 July 1840.
201 *It is indeed shocking to think:* Poland, pp. v–vi.
201 *a very erroneous test:* ibid., pp. 16–17.
201 *the most trifling action of human life:* ibid., p. 76.
202 *the robbery part of this dreadful deed was so clumsy:* Sir Robert
　　　Adair to Lord G. William Russell, 12 May 1840, *LGWR,* vol. 3,
　　　p. 299.
203 *I never heard a very little from him:* Hobler, seq. 150.
204 *I do not know of his having any female acquaintance:* ibid.,
　　　seq. 141.
204 *deceased wore a truss . . . he had had some slight struggle: The
　　　Times,* 7 May 1840.

205 *completely saturated with gore:* Henry Elsgood's testimony at the Bow Street committal hearing, *The Times*, 23 May 1840.

207 *involuntary at the time death took place:* John Nussey's testimony at the Bow Street committal hearing, *The Times*, 23 May 1840.

208 *apparently sane:* Wikipedia entry for Edward Oxford, quoting Broadmoor Hospital case file, 1864, en.wikipedia.org.

208 *a woman of loose character: The Times*, 11 May 1840.

Select Bibliography

Atlay, James, *Famous Trials of the Century* (London, 1899)

Ballantine, William, *Some Experiences of a Barrister's Life* (2 vols., London, 1882)

Barham, R. H. D., *The Life and Letters of the Rev. Richard Harris Barham, Author of the Ingoldsby Legends: With a Selection from His Miscellaneous Poems* (2 vols., London, 1870)

Benson, A. C., and Esher, R. B. B. (eds.), *The Letters of Queen Victoria: A Selection from Her Majesty's Correspondence between the Years 1837 and 1861* (3 vols., London, 1911)

Blakiston, Georgiana, *Lord William Russell and His Wife, 1815–1846* (London, 1972)

Bleakley, Horace, *Jack Sheppard in Literature and Drama*, with an epilogue by S. M. Ellis (London, 1933)

Bridges, Yseult, *Two Studies in Crime: The Murder of Lord William Russell and the Murder of Julia Wallace* (London, 1959)

Buckstone, J. B., *Jack Sheppard: A Drama in Four Acts* (London, 1839)

Burnett, John, *Useful Toil: Autobiographies of Working People from the 1820s to the 1920s* (London, 1974)

Christian, E. E. [Eleanor Emma Picken], "Reminiscences of Charles Dickens from a Young Lady's Diary," *Englishwoman's Domestic Magazine* (June 1871), issue 78, pp. 336–44

——, "Recollections of Charles Dickens," *Temple Bar: With Which is Incorporated Bentley's Miscellany* (April 1888), pp. 481–506

Collins, Philip, *Dickens and Crime* (London, 1964)

Courtney, Janet, *The Adventurous Thirties: A Chapter in the Women's Movement* (Oxford, 1933)

Curl, J. S., *The Victorian Celebration of Death* (Newton Abbot, 1972)

Elliotson, John, *Illustrations of Phrenology: Courvoisier* (London, 1841)

Ellis, S. M., *William Harrison Ainsworth and His Friends* (2 vols., London, 1911)

Field, B. (ed.), *The Memoirs of James Hardy Vaux, Written by Himself* (London, 1827)

Fisher, D. R. (ed.), *The History of Parliament: The House of Commons 1820–1832* (Cambridge, 2009)

Flanders, Judith, *The Invention of Murder: How the Victorians Revelled in Death and Detection and Created Modern Crime* (London, 2011)

Fremantle, Anne (ed.), *The Wynne Diaries* (3 vols., London, 1935)

Frewen, Moreton, *Melton Mowbray, and Other Memories* (London, 1924)

Gatrell, V. A. C., *The Hanging Tree: Execution and the English People 1770–1868* (Oxford, 1994)

Goodman, Walter, *The Keeleys on the Stage and at Home* (London, 1895)

Gore, John, *Nelson's Hardy and His Wife: Some Account of the Lives and Married Life of Vice-Admiral Sir Thomas Masterman Hardy, G.C.B. and of His Wife, Louisa, Lady Hardy, Derived from the Hitherto Unpublished Journals* (London, 1935)

Grant, James, *Portraits of Public Characters*, (2 vols., London, 1841)

Hanchant, W. L. [Wilfred Lewis] (ed.), *The Newgate Garland or Flowers of Hemp* (London, 1932)

Henderson, Emily, *Recollections of the Public Career and Private Life of the Late John Adolphus, the Eminent Barrister and Historian, with Extracts from His Diaries* (London, 1871)

Hibbard, Addison (ed.), *The Book of Poe* (New York, 1934)

Hobler, Francis, "An Account of the Murder of the Lord William Russell on the Night of the 5th & 6th May 1840," Harvard Law School Library, MS 4487

Hollingsworth, Keith, *The Newgate Novel, 1830–1847: Bulwer, Ainsworth, Dickens & Thackeray* (Detroit, 1963)

Horne, R. H., *A New Spirit of the Age* (2 vols., London, 1844)

House, Madeline, Storey, Graham, et al., *The Pilgrim Edition of the Letters of Charles Dickens* (12 vols., Oxford, 1965–2002)

Hudson, Ronald, et al. (eds.), *The Brownings' Correspondence* (24 vols., London, 1984–)

Ilchester, Earl of (ed.), *The Letters of Elizabeth, Lady Holland to Her Son, 1821–1845* (London, 1946)

Jalland, Patricia, *Death in the Victorian Family* (Oxford, 1996)

Jerrold, Blanchard (ed.), *The Best of All Good Company* (London, 1871)

John, Juliet (ed.), *Cult Criminals: The Newgate Novels 1830–47* (6 vols., London, 1998): vol. 1, Edward Bulwer-Lytton, *Paul Clifford;* vol. 2, Edward Bulwer-Lytton, *Eugene Aram;* vol. 5, William Harrison Ainsworth, *Rookwood;* vol. 6, William Harrison Ainsworth, *Jack Sheppard*

John S. Farmer's Canting Songs and Slang Rhymes, www.fromold books.org

Kelley, P., and Hudson, R. (eds.), *The Brownings' Correspondence* (5 vols., London, 1984–)

Kitton, Frederic G., *Charles Dickens by Pen and Pencil* (London, 1889)

Letters to Lord G. William Russell from Various Writers 1817–1845 (3 vols., London, 1915)

Miller, Betty (ed.), *Elizabeth Barrett to Miss Mitford: Letters of Elizabeth Barrett Browning to Mary Russell Mitford* (London, 1954)

Ormond, Richard, *Sir Edwin Landseer* (London, 1981)

Pearce, Edward (ed.), *The Diaries of Charles Greville* (London, 2005)

Picard, Liza, *Victorian London: The Life of a City 1840–1870* (London, 2005)

Pigot and Co.'s London & Provincial New Commercial Directory (London, 1840)

Poland, Sir H. (ed.), *Report of the Trial of Courvoisier for the Murder of Lord William Russell, June 1840* (London, 1918)

Pope, Willard Bissell (ed.), *Diary of Benjamin Robert Haydon* (Cambridge, Mass., 1963)

Priestman, Martin, *Detective Fiction and Literature* (London, 1990)

Ray, Gordon N. (ed.), *The Letters and Private Papers of William Makepeace Thackeray* (4 vols., London, 1946)

Russell of Liverpool, Lord, *Though the Heavens Fall* (London, 1956)

Sencicle, Lorraine, *Banking on Dover* (Dover, 1993)

Slater, Michael, *Charles Dickens* (New Haven, 2011)

Taylor, D. J., *Thackeray* (London, 1999)

Thackeray, William Makepeace, *Catherine: A Story by Ikey Solomons, Esq, Junior*, ed. Sheldon F. Goldfarb (Ann Arbor, Mich., 1999)

Thackeray, William Makepeace, "Going to See a Man Hanged," *Fraser's Magazine* (August 1840)

[Thackeray, William Makepeace], "Horae Catnachianae: A Dissertation on Ballads, with a Few Unnecessary Remarks on Jonathan Wild, John Sheppard, Paul Clifford, and—Fagin, Esqrs.," *Fraser's Magazine*, 19 (April 1839), pp. 407–24

Thompson, Dave, *Fierce Fiction: Dickens, Ainsworth, Bulwer and Thackeray in the Shadows of Newgate Prison* (Davethompson books.com, 2009)

Tomalin, Claire, *Charles Dickens: A Life* (London, 2011)

Toynbee, William (ed.), *The Diaries of William Charles Macready, 1833–1851* (2 vols., London, 1912)

Woodberry, George Edward, *The Life of Edgar Allan Poe, with His Chief Correspondence with Men of Letters* (New York, 1965)

Yates, E. H. (ed.), *Celebrities at Home* (London, 1879)

Acknowledgements

I first became aware of the Russell murder while reading newspapers of the time during my research into the life of Charlotte Brontë; its interest to Dickens and Thackeray also became apparent while I was writing that book. It would have been very difficult to discover more about either the crime or the *Jack Sheppard* controversy, though, without the remarkable resources offered by the digitization of many contemporary newspapers and periodicals, and I would like to express my gratitude to all the unnamed data managers, digitizers and editors responsible for sites such as British Newspapers Online, *The Times* Digital Archive and Gale Cengage Learning. They have been essential and constantly surprising resources in my research.

In the material world, several individual members of staff at libraries and other institutions have generously given me their time and professional expertise, and I would particularly like to thank the staff of the Bodleian Library, British Library, Harvard Law School Library, Sotheby's and London Metropolitan Archive, Naomi Tiley of Balliol College Library, Lianne Smith at Brasenose College Library, Victoria Poulton and Natasha Kikas at Woburn Abbey Archive and Louise Baker at Madame Tussauds, who managed to find the company's 1840 catalogue, even during a removal of all the stock.

At Viking Penguin, I would like to thank my editors Venetia Butterfield and Isabel Wall and copy-editor Caroline Pretty for all their work on the text. I would also like to thank Sara Granger in Production, Pete Pawsey for his help with the images, and Jane Gentle in Publicity. On the New York side of the production, I am much indebted to Kris Puopolo, who has proved as astute and careful a reader and editor as ever, and to Daniel Meyer, her assistant at Alfred A. Knopf, also to page designer Betty Lew and to Kathy Zuckerman, a wonderful publicist. My agent Geri Thoma has again been immensely supportive at every stage of composition, from first thoughts to finished copy; my thanks to her, and to Andrea Morrison of Writers House.

I'm very grateful to all the friends who have taken an interest in this project and listened patiently to the emerging details of this long-ago mystery, including those at La Maison Verte in Roujan in the summer of 2017, who heard a great deal about it in rudimentary form, and my dear friends Annie Bartlett and Sandra Evans, whose expert witness, 177 years after the event, was extremely pertinent to my understanding of how throats behave when cut. Thanks also to Juliet Brown and Kate Bailey for helping us to reconstruct the crime on an Umbrian terrace.

Thanks are also due to my sister Suzanne Challacombe, who very kindly helped me with François Courvoisier's idiosyncratic French, to Lorraine Sencicle and Liza Picard for answers to specific questions, to Zoe Waldie for her invaluable support and encouragement all along the way, and to Paul Strohm, who has, as ever, been the ideal listener, enthusiast and advice-giver throughout an intense year of reading and writing.

Index

Illustration Credits

Map: Mayfair in 1830, detail from a map of London by C. & J. Greenwood; Harvard University Map Collection, G5754-L7-1830-G7

14 Norfolk Street: Harvard Law School Library, Trials Broadsides 472, seq 187; Historical & Special Collections, Harvard Law School Library

Newspaper illustration: Harvard Law School Library, Trials Broadsides 472, seq 192; Historical & Special Collections, Harvard Law School Library

Broadside poster: Harvard Law School Library, Trials Broadsides 472, seq 186; Historical & Special Collections, Harvard Law School Library

Ainsworth: William Harrison Ainsworth by William Greatbach, after Richard James Lane, NPG D21947, © National Portrait Gallery, London

Dickens: Charles Dickens by Samuel Laurence, 1838, NPG 5207, © National Portrait Gallery, London

Thackeray: William Makepeace Thackeray by Frank Stone, 1839, NPG 4210, © National Portrait Gallery, London

Keeley: Wikimedia Commons

Sheet music: George Cruikshank, cover of the sheet music for 'Nix My Dolly, Pals, Fake Away', Cruik 1839.7.183-q, Graphic Arts Division, Department of Rare Books and Special Collections, Princeton University Library

"The March of Knowledge": *The Penny Satirist*, 14 December 1839, Gale Cengage Learning, document number DX1901077596

Attempted assassination: Edward Oxford's assassination attempt
on Queen Victoria by G. H. Miles, 1840, Alamy
Raven: Free Library of Philadelphia
Sketch of Courvoisier: Harvard Law School Library MS 4487, seq
359; Historical & Special Collections, Harvard Law School
Library
Courvoisier in Newgate: Harvard Law School Library, Trials
Broadsides 472, seq 266; Historical & Special Collections, Har-
vard Law School Library
Death mask: © Madame Tussauds Archives

Claire Harman is the author of *Charlotte Brontë: A Fiery Heart; Sylvia Townsend Warner,* for which she won the John Llewellyn Rhys Prize; biographies of Fanny Burney and Robert Louis Stevenson; and *Jane's Fame: How Jane Austen Conquered the World.* She is a fellow of the Royal Society of Literature and a frequent reviewer. She divides her time between New York City and Oxford, England.

A NOTE ON THE TYPE

This book was set in Old Style No. 7. This face is largely based on a series originally cut by the Bruce Foundry in the early 1870s, and that face, in its turn, appears to have followed in all essentials the details of a face designed and cut some years before by the celebrated Edinburgh typefounders Miller & Richard.

Composed by North Market Street Graphics,
Lancaster, Pennsylvania

Printed and bound by Berryville Graphics,
Berryville, Virginia

Designed by Betty Lew